Facial Recognition

Facial Recognition

Mark Andrejevic
and Neil Selwyn

polity

First published in 2022 by Polity Press

Polity Press
65 Bridge Street
Cambridge CB2 1UR, UK

Polity Press
111 River Street
Hoboken, NJ 07030, USA

ISBN-13: 978-1-5095-4732-6
ISBN-13: 978-1-5095-4733-3(pb)

A catalogue record for this book is available from the British Library.

Library of Congress Control Number: 2022930699

Typeset in 10.5 on 13pt Sabon
by Fakenham Prepress Solutions, Fakenham, Norfolk NR21 8NL
Printed and bound in the UK by CPI Group (UK) Ltd, Croydon

The publisher has used its best endeavours to ensure that the URLs for external websites referred to in this book are correct and active at the time of going to press. However, the publisher has no responsibility for the websites and can make no guarantee that a site will remain live or that the content is or will remain appropriate.

Every effort has been made to trace all copyright holders, but if any have been overlooked the publisher will be pleased to include any necessary credits in any subsequent reprint or edition.

For further information on Polity, visit our website:
politybooks.com

Contents

Acknowledgements

The issues we address in the following pages have come to public attention through the efforts of many people whose work we draw upon to write this book – including Ruha Benjamin, Joy Buolamwini, Kelly Gates, Timnit Gebru, Chris Gilliard, Woodrow Hartzog, Os Keyes, Safiya Noble, Deborah Raji, Evan Selinger, Luke Stark, Simone Browne and many others. We look forward to the books that these (and other) critics are writing on this topic. Our book offers an initial perspective on a topic that is being worked on by hundreds of critically minded and concerned people.

The writing of this book arises as part of a research project funded by the Australian Research Council (DP200100189). We would especially like to thank our co-researchers Chris O'Neill, Gavin Smith and Xin Gu for all their ongoing conversations around these issues, as well as other research colleagues including Liz Campbell, Robbie Fordyce, Zala Volcic, Miguel Vatter and Brett Hutchins.

We are also grateful to the industry, regulatory and computer science experts who have spoken with us as part of the ARC research project, taking time to explain the intricacies of the facial recognition industry and how this technology is being implemented in everyday society.

Preface

The human visual system is remarkably good at recognizing faces. It is estimated that most adults are capable of recognizing around 5,000 different faces, taking an average of around 0.2 seconds to work out who someone is. A very small number of individuals are exceptionally good at remembering the faces of different people they come across. These 'super-recognizers' can recall up to 80 per cent of the faces they see (as compared to the 20 per cent level that most people are capable of) and are highly sought after by police, intelligence agencies, banks and casinos to provide specialist face identification. Nevertheless, even the most capable human is unable to maintain this level of recognition over prolonged periods of time, nor to expand their recognitive abilities to the scale of entire national populations. The attempt to recognize individuals at this scale has been an ongoing project that – like so much else – has recently been adopted by the developers of automated digital technology. For the first time in human history, we are confronting the prospect of systems that would have the capacity to recognize individuals by automatically comparing them to databases on the scale of national populations – and beyond.

Computer-based facial recognition carries with it the promise of the infallible and all-insightful eyewitness account. This is the compelling power of 'seeing' something happen and knowing exactly who is involved, even if we require a camera to do the seeing and a computer to do the recognizing. Because this technology relies on the unblinking eye of the machine, it also ushers in the prospect of always-on, ubiquitous identification at-a-distance – the ability to augment the world around us with a 'recognitive' overlay. In this regard, facial recognition technology marks a decisive shift in monitoring capability, promising the advent of spaces that recognize us wherever we go, even if the people around us do not. We might describe this as the definitive end of a certain kind of privacy. Perhaps, once upon a time, it was reasonable to presume that we retained some anonymity in public spaces, with the majority of our actions and activities going unremarked and unrecorded. If so, then the widespread use of facial recognition-enabled cameras marks the end of such a time.

In many ways, it might seem surprising that such technology would gain widespread purchase, given the demonstrable threat to privacy and concerns about accuracy and bias. However, the experience of the past couple of decades has been shaped by the widespread implementation of increasingly comprehensive and granular forms of monitoring in exchange for the convenience and affordances of various data-driven digital technologies. The ever-growing forms of surveillance and 'dataveillance' associated with the use of smartphones and social media have been well documented and discussed. In light of these general conditions, it would be surprising if we collectively ended up deciding to finally and definitively draw the line at facial recognition technology. 'Go ahead and track wherever I go, all of my communications and online interactions, everything I look at, write, do or share online . . . just don't scan my face.'

Drawing on the lessons of the recent past and, in particular, the rise of the online surveillance economy, this book starts from the premise that various forms of facial recognition technology will likely become steadily embedded in the minutiae of daily life. In a practical sense, numerous facial recognition applications already exist to allow us to unlock our phones without having to key in any numbers or to provide cardless, touchless access to mass transit, ATM machines, offices, homes and cars. In a more abstract sense, this is technology that promises to give us the satisfaction (at least to some) of recognition – a feeling that the places through which we move know us and respond to us personally, as is increasingly the case in online spaces. In some ways, then, this is technology that offers us the comforting sense that we make an impression. Moreover, as with other recognition-based interactive technologies, the lure of facial recognition technology comes with the promise of convenience, efficiency *and* comfort. This is technology that is framed by its proponents as the solution to inconvenience, inefficiency and risk in a variety of contexts. In the friction-free world envisioned by proselytizers of the technology, for example, face recognition opens up a world of convenience: cars that open at a glance and automatically adjust the seat, mirrors and soundtrack to suit the driver; shops without checkout queues; speedy transit through borders and checkpoints of all kinds, from international customs to secure office spaces (no more key cards!).

For those on the less privileged side of this technology, however, recognition is not necessarily a benefit. This is technology that can be used to track those who fall under suspicion, to bar access, to scrutinize and to sort. This is also technology that the IT industry is currently attempting to develop in forms that can assess someone's employability, potential threat and/or creditworthiness. In this respect, facial recognition technology may usher in yet another dimension of the digital divide – significant disparities between those who use and control the technology as opposed to those who are subjected to it. As we shall see throughout this book, there are numerous instances where such disparities are already beginning to emerge – from casino managers using facial recognition to decide which patrons get filtered into fast-track VIP queues through to authoritarian states using facial recognition technology to identify and track ethnic minorities.

Yet proponents of FRT are quick to reason that we should not lose sight of more positive uses of the technology, such as deployment of the technology to reunite missing children with their families. In 2020, facial recognition was used to reunite Mao Yin from Xi'an with the birth parents from whom he had been kidnapped 32 years earlier. Authorities reportedly used a photo of the child to create a simulated image of what he would look like as an adult and then searched for matches using facial recognition technology. Elsewhere, researchers have explored the use of facial recognition technology to identify families separated by natural disasters, even if they have sustained facial injuries. These examples are deployed by advocates of the technology to highlight its real pro-social uses.

Those in favour of FRT would also point to uses that many support for increased security: the ability to identify criminals who might otherwise have escaped the consequences of their actions; or helping to prevent fraud that costs people tens of billions of dollars a year. These forms of facial recognition technology speak to the feeling of frustration that comes with the uncertainty that can plague law enforcement: the strong suspicion that someone must be guilty while being unable to find them, and/or the need to know for sure whether a guilty verdict is fully justified. Whether or not facial recognition technology can follow through on the promise to provide certainty is, however, a different matter. As we shall see, there is no such thing as completely certain identification when it comes to automated face matching. Moreover, this is technology that has long been plagued by issues of misrecognition and bias, rendering it less reliable for certain populations. While some experts might argue that such flaws have all been eliminated, others suggest that it is, even in theory, impossible to eradicate entirely.

So, all told, this is technology that appears in many guises: from authoritarian control to personal assistant. As in the case of technology more generally, its future will depend on how we choose to use it, and who the 'we' end up being. One thing seems clear: this is technology that is likely to become more widespread in the near future, which means the time to anticipate and assess its social consequences is now.

1

Facial Recognition: An Introduction

Introduction

The beginning of the 2020s marked a point when facial recognition technology was thrust to the forefront of political and mainstream concern. This was a time when some of the most high-profile tech companies vowed to suspend their development of the technology, or else cease operations completely. In the midst of the 2020 Black Lives Matter protests in the United States against police brutality, CEO Arvind Krishna sent an open letter to Congress pledging that 'IBM no longer offers general purpose IBM facial recognition or analysis software' (IBM 2020). Soon after, Amazon joined Microsoft in also announcing that it was 'implementing a one-year moratorium on police use of Amazon's facial recognition technology' (Amazon 2020). Twelve months later, these corporate stances were reaffirmed, and various US city, state and federal bans on government use of facial recognition technology (FRT) were pursued. Then, towards the end of 2021 Facebook proclaimed that it was switching off the FRT auto-tagging feature on the social media platform, and deleting its vast dataset of over one billion facial scans in response to what it framed as 'many concerns about the place of facial recognition technology in society' (Hill and Mac 2021).

Perhaps the most damning indictment came from within the academic computer science community. The ACM (Association for Computing Machinery), while hardly the most politically motivated or publicity-seeking organization, issued a sternly worded 'statement on principles and pre-requisites for the development, evaluation and use of unbiased facial recognition technologies'. This June 2020 statement pulled no punches:

> when rigorously evaluated, the technology too often produces results demonstrating clear bias based on ethnic, racial, gender, and other human characteristics recognizable by computer systems. . . . Such bias and its effects are scientifically and socially unacceptable . . . [the committee] urges an immediate suspension of the current and future private and governmental use of facial recognition technologies in all circumstances known or reasonably foreseeable to be prejudicial to established human and legal rights. (ACM 2020)

These statements and actions were welcomed at the time by activists and critics as marking the end of what had come in some circles to represent a fundamentally oppressive, discriminatory and retrograde aspect of digital technology development. Nevertheless, as with any multi-billion-dollar industry based on cutting-edge technology development, the story is not so simple.

Soon after their announcements, many of the Big Tech companies began to face challenges over the details of their apparent changes of heart. What exactly did IBM mean by 'general purpose' facial recognition, and what other specific purposes did that leave open? Amazon only offered to suspend police use of its Rekognition technology, while proudly boasting that it would continue with its humanitarian uses by other organizations. Most of the US city bans on facial recognition were directed at specific uses by municipal services. Even the ACM statement was actually a call for improving the accuracy, transparency and accountability of what it acknowledged was 'powerful' technology that was 'likely to improve in the future' with 'potential to help meet significant societal needs'. By placing concerns around bias at the heart of the push-back against the technology, some bans served as an incitement to further develop the technology and provided it with a potential alibi: if this technology could be developed without systematic forms of bias, then perhaps it might be acceptable.

Similarly, the high-profile Facebook promise to delete its vast dataset of facial recognition scans deflected attention from the fact that the company was retaining the DeepFace model that it had developed from this dataset, and plans to incorporate FRT into future products including its plans for the 'metaverse' and for smart glasses – stressing that 'every new technology brings with it potential for both benefit and concern, and we want to find the right balance' (Hill and Mac 2021). Proclamations such as this are best seen as Big Tech companies 'responding to the controversy by pivoting rather than pulling back' (Bass and Bergen 2021). Investment in facial recognition ventures continues to rise, US companies continue to sell facial recognition products to police and security forces overseas, as well as develop less controversial domestic markets.

So, while industry acknowledgement of the need to reconsider the use of facial recognition technology was welcome, this seemingly significant turning-point has subsequently proved to make little difference to the ongoing rise of this technology around the world. A well-crafted proposal to Congress – the Facial Recognition and Biometric Technology Moratorium Act – for federal legislation that sought to place an indefinite ban on police use of the technology received no industry support, and eventually sank without trace. At the same time, the development and implementation of FRT continued apace. As it turned out, the opening years of the 2020s proved to be a time when FRT was introduced into everything from $400 home security camera systems through to 'pay-by-face' kiosks in burger chains. A couple of months after the Amazon and ACM announcements, it was estimated that the market for 'facial biometrics' would exceed US$15billion by 2027 (Burt 2020).

Against this background, this book attempts to make sense of one of the most far-reaching – and controversial – technologies of recent times. How did we reach a point where the *New York Times* shifted from enthusing in 2008 that 'Facial recognition software holds great promise' (*New York Times* 2008) to presenting 'A Case for Banning Facial Recognition' (*New York Times* 2020a) just over a decade later? How do controversies over the use of this technology for law enforcement compare with more banal applications in shopping malls and sports stadia, and with humanitarian uses such as for finding missing children? We take these seemingly disparate applications of the technology to be held together by what Kelly Gates describes as a shared logic of control based on increasingly comprehensive monitoring and individualization. As she puts it in her groundbreaking work on facial recognition technology:

> the possibility of digital biometric identification should not be understood in narrow terms as the natural outgrowth of technical advancements in identification systems. Instead, these technologies are being envisioned and designed to fulfil certain perceived social necessities and political–economic demands of large-scale, late capitalist societies . . . The expansion of computer networks has created new problems of communication-without-bodies, necessitating new techniques for identifying people, verifying their legitimate identities, and otherwise gaining knowledge about who they are. (Gates 2011: 16)

In this opening chapter, we consider how this once niche 'biometric' technology grew to be a relatively inexpensive and easy 'plug-in' to even the most innocuous everyday devices and applications. First, we look back over the history of computers being given the task of matching faces with people – an application that computer scientists have been grappling with since the 1960s. This history is an important part of making sense of the present and future uses of this technology, with a number of logics already set in motion well before this technology came to mainstream public attention. We then set the scene for the rest of the book by considering the social implications of how this technology is currently being used, as well as the future applications that lie ahead. More significantly, perhaps, we begin to consider the promised benefits and overarching imperatives that shape the current deployment of the technology. Despite highly publicized concerns and backlash, FRT continues to develop apace and is poised to transform the surveillance landscape. Why is it that despite recent controversies, the technology nonetheless continues to work its way into so many aspects of contemporary technology and its anticipated future uses?

A history of computers and facial recognition

1960s to 1990s: establishing a technical proof of concept

The association between computers and facial recognition is usually traced back to the work of US researcher Woodrow (Woody) Wilson Bledsoe and his collaborators Helen Chan Wolf and Charles Bisson. These three spent much of the 1960s working under the guise of the Panoramic Research company based in Palo Alto. Previously, Bledsoe had been involved in developing the 'n-tuple' approach to automated pattern recognition – a technique that divides images of shapes onto a grid of cells, assigning values of 1 (full) and 0 (empty) to each pixel, and then computing a unique score that could be later matched to other close-scoring patterns. Extending this logic, the Panoramic team saw faces as a

computationally challenging (in Bledsoe's words, 'noisy')
pattern to match.

That said, Bledsoe's interest in face matching was driven
by broader ambitions. In a detailed investigative report on
Panoramic Research over fifty years later, journalist Shaun
Raviv (2020) recounted Bledsoe's innocuous ambitions
for expanding this technology beyond merely recognizing
patterns, and instead building a mechanic 'computer friend':
'I could see it, or a part of it, in a small camera that would fit
on my glasses, with an attached earplug that would whisper
into my ear the names of my friends and acquaintances as I
met them on the street . . . For you see, my computer friend
had the ability to recognize faces.'

In this formulation, Bledsoe touches on a characteristic
theme of facial recognition technology that highlights both its
appeal and its 'creep factor'. The idea that the computerized
automated interfaces that increasingly populate our interactive world might come to recognize us certainly makes the
technology feel less alienating – especially the idea that this
is technology capable of getting to 'know' us. In a world
where we spend more and more time 'at the interface', many
people feel an implicit desire to humanize the technologies
that surround us – partly in an attempt to make our digitally
mediated lives a bit less isolating. At the same time, of
course, there is something uncanny, alarming, and creepy
about machines that seem to recognize us and divulge our
identities – in part because this endows them with an opaque
power. This is technology that may know our details while
what goes on behind the interface remains obscure to any
onlooker. What does the machine know, what information
is it collecting and whom is it sharing it? There is always
something suspect lurking in the promise of machinic recognition: a pastiche of human interaction.

Panoramic, however, took a more pragmatic approach than
that outlined by Bledsoe, pitching the technology's capability
for a variety of military intelligence and law enforcement
applications. For the remainder of the 1960s, nearly all the

company's work took the form of classified projects funded by a succession of unspecified US intelligence agencies. Bledsoe's initial proposal to conduct 'a study to determine the feasibility of a simplified facial recognition machine' was necessarily small-scale – seeking to program a computer to recognize ten different faces. When it became apparent that this feat could not be achieved by the computer alone, the Panoramic team adopted a 'man-machine' approach with human operators using electronic tablets to manually mark coordinates of various facial features including the eyes, nose, hairline and mouth. This data could then be transformed with the n-tuple methods. While progress was slow, by 1967 Panoramic researchers had successfully developed a system that could match police mugshots within a photographic database of '400 adult male Caucasians'. The initial proof of concept for facial recognition had been achieved.

Bedsloe's work established many of the basic principles that facial recognition developers continue to develop fifty years later, while also encountering many of the field's enduring problems. For example, the Panoramic team established the idea of digitizing images and using pointillistic methods, as well as making early attempts to rotate images to account for head tilt, lean and rotation. More fundamentally, even the most sophisticated facial recognition systems continue Bledsoe's basic approach of creating scores for images and comparing similarities. The Panoramic team also encountered now-familiar challenges to facial recognition developers – such as dealing with variations in facial expression, hair growth and the effects of aging, as well as how photographs are lit and composed.

Perhaps more significantly, Bedsloe also unwittingly pre-empted much of the ethical and moral complexities of this new branch of computer science. Panoramic took regular funding from various state agencies for highly classified applications of facial recognition. Although Panoramic pitched a Defence Department project in 1965 to use facial recognition to identify people's racial background, little interest tended to be shown in training their systems to recognize diverse sets of images. As Raviv (2020) notes, 'I did not see images of women or people of colour, or references to them, in any of Woody's facial-recognition studies.' Bledsoe's dream of an all-seeing 'computer friend' was already mired in the realities of 1960s US society and politics.

These initial efforts were then followed by a succession of US research and development projects over the next thirty years. A paper in May 1971 by Jay Goldstein, Leon Harman and Ann Lesk (all engineers at Bell Telephone Laboratories) outlined a refined method for manual facial recognition relying on 22 key 'markers'. These included features such as ear protrusion and eyebrow separation – with the team estimating that being able to match as few as seven of these markers could result in a match for unique identification. As with Bledsoe's work, this was a 'man-machine' system relying on researchers manually marking photographs. Again, all the examples given (including their composite 'Mr. Average' image) were white middle-aged men.

These techniques continued to be refined over the 1970s and 1980s, with researchers using larger training datasets and becoming less reliant on manual coding. Using an expanded set of 850 digitized photographs, the Japanese researcher Takeo Kanade was soon able to program the automated extraction of key facial features such as eyes, mouth and nose. Further refinements continued up until the end of the 1980s when Lawrence Sirovich and Michael Kirby – mathematicians from Brown University – made what is now considered to be a significant breakthrough. This involved the use of a linear algebra technique called 'eigenvectors' to produce a relatively small 'basis set' of low-dimensional face images ('eigenfaces'). These eigenface images were composite images of hundreds of actual faces, resulting in blurry low-resolution patterns, which often look little like recognizable faces.

Sirovich and Kirby reasoned that any human face could be uniquely identified by its variation from a baseline

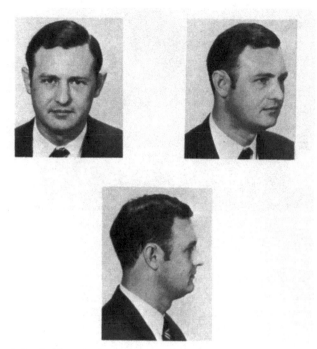

Figure 1.1   Goldstein, Harmon and Lesk's (1971) profile photographs of an 'average' face. © IEEE

'average face' eigenface and the extent to which its features are present in other eigenface images. Significantly, Sirovich and Kirby found that most people could be identified on the basis of how their face matched with fewer than one hundred of these eigenface images. The advantage of this approach was that it could recognize and store an individual's face as a series of values corresponding to each of the 'basis set' eigenfaces being used in the system. Relying on numbers rather than digital photographs meant that massive amounts of facial information could be collated and stored.

A few years later, these efficiencies allowed Alex Pentland and Matthew Turk from MIT's Media Lab to refine the eigenface technique to extract images of human faces from

Figure 1.2 'Average face' based on ensemble of 115 faces (Sirovich and Kirby 1987). Reprinted with permission from © The Optical Society.

their background environments, and then make quick matches. Three decades on from Bledsoe's original plans, a working system for real-time automatic facial detection had been realized. As Turk and Pentland (1991) put it, their development of the eigenface approach 'was motivated by information theory, leading to the idea of basing face recognition on a small set of image features that best approximate the set of known face images, without requiring that they correspond to our intuitive notions of facial parts and features'. This move away from having to recognize a 'face' per se was acknowledged to be 'a practical solution that is well fitted to the problem of face recognition. It is fast, relatively simple, and has been shown to work well in a somewhat constrained environment.'

1990s to 2010s: establishing commercial opportunities

With these technical precedents having been set, attention then shifted to developing a commercial market for facial recognition technology. Central to these efforts in the United States were the government agencies DARPA (the Defence Advanced Research Projects Agency) and NIST (the National Institute of Standards and Technology). These agencies collaborated during the 1990s to run the FERET (Face Recognition Technology) research program, with the goal of collating a large database of high-quality images for commercial developers to use. NIST subsequently launched a program to provide independent government evaluations of commercial facial recognition systems from the time they were being developed or through to their entry into the commercial market. These Face Recognition Vendor Tests were held four times during the 2000s, alongside a couple of Face Recognition Grand Challenges – all designed to encourage the development of increasingly accurate and adaptable systems.

Despite this extensive government support, facial recognition remained a frustratingly inconsistent and unreliable technology throughout the 2000s. The computational challenges inherent in the process of extracting and processing large numbers of potential facial images meant that facial recognition systems remained difficult to deploy at scale. One notable setback was the 2001 covert deployment of facial recognition at Super Bowl XXXV in Tampa. Here federal authorities and state police monitored the stadium and surrounding bars and clubs as a test case for the FaceFinder large-scale surveillance system. While claiming success in detecting 19 known 'petty criminals' from around 100,000 attendees, no arrests were made, and there was a general sense that the system had proven incapable of coping with large crowds. Public reaction to what news media soon dubbed the 'Snooper Bowl' remained muted.

Yet, after forty years of incremental progress, the technological development that eventually tipped facial recognition over into being reliable and powerful enough to be deployed at scale was not directly related to computer vision or pattern matching per se. Instead, one of the most significant shifts in facial recognition was the rise of social media platforms such as Myspace and the appropriately named Facebook. In particular, one unforeseen consequence of people's insatiable appetite for sharing images of themselves on social media (at all angles, and all states of appearance) was facial recognition developers being gifted an unprecedented corpus of billions of facial images and associated identifying data. Coupled with advances in computer vision technology and machine learning techniques, the 2010s proved to be the decade in which the 'grand challenge' of facial recognition looked likely to be achieved. Even as the 2020s progress, sporadic social media viral challenges such as *#MeAt20* and *#10YearChallenge* continue to be initiated as thinly veiled efforts to add to training data for further refining facial analysis and matching software. In many ways, the persistence of 'selfie culture' has hastened the deployment of facial recognition into most aspects of our everyday lives. The avalanche of images that perhaps carry some fleeting interest to those who take them, come to serve as a valuable enduring resource for automated systems. It is almost as if, in our hypermediated culture, we are posing for the machine.

Indeed, as far as most developers are concerned, the technical advancement of facial recognition looks set to continue with pace throughout the 2020s. Alongside the glut of photographs now available on social media (as well as massive image datasets now being produced and collated by government and industry sources), a number of other factors are driving these advances. From a technical point of view, we are now seeing rapid advances in computer processing speeds, the rise of cloud-based data storage, as well as machine learning developments in 'deep convolutional neural networks'. From the human side of things, the facial recognition industry benefits from the rise of cheap online 'gig' labour, with large numbers of low-paid micro workers now paid to manually identify and tag facial features for a few cents per click. All told, the technical, economic and cultural conditions are now set for the large-scale realization of what Bledsoe, Wolf, Sirovich started 50 years earlier.

What does the history of facial recognition tell us?

Overviews of FRT will often gloss over these early decades as something of a curiosity. Yet, in order to make full sense of any technology it is crucial to pay attention to these precedents. While, as Adrian Daub (2020: 3) notes, the IT industry is a place 'that likes to pretend its ideas don't have any history', there is much that can be taken from this relatively slow unfolding of FRT from the 1960s through to the 2010s.

First and foremost, is the primary focus on FRT as a computational exercise. In contrast to current ongoing debates over the rights and wrongs of deploying FRT across various parts of society, these early years saw facial recognition framed mainly in terms of the technical challenge of getting a computer to recognize a face – with little evident regard for broader social consequences. As such, the efforts of facial recognition developers between the 1960s and 2010s remained focused firmly on issues of technical efficiency – nudging the accuracy of their systems from 70 to 80 to 90 per cent and beyond, achieving faster speeds and lower frame rates. The early manual coding of facial features and filling in cells as either a '1' or a '0' neatly illustrate this idea of facial recognition as a data-driven exercise – focused predominantly on mathematics rather than people. In this sense, the face is simply a prompt for assigning scores, producing a series of numbers, and engaging in complex mathematical matching exercises. As Sirovich and Kirby (1987: 522) put it, 'a face, or for that matter any object, can be regarded as a pointwise map of reflectivities'.

The past fifty years certainly illustrate how this numerical lens leads to a distinct set of assumptions about faces, people and the act of recognition. For example, the idea of an 'average' face makes far better sense in terms of statistics than in social or biological terms. If one sees the face as an informatically 'noisy' data object, then this leads on to an implicit acceptance of errors and statistical bias. Indeed, this history also illustrates that – as with any data-related exercise – facial recognition is not embarked on as an exact science. Rather, this history of research and development points to the essentially de-socialized and dehumanized nature of the endeavour of facial recognition. Lila Lee-Morrison describes this as a 'mechanic' way of approaching the face that is rooted in a 'deterritorialization' of visual perception, where the act of perception is freed from the person doing the seeing and the person being seen. This results in entirely new meanings being produced that are based on 'abstract and mathematically based caricatures' (Lee-Morrison 2019: 84) rather than any human understandings of what a face is and how it is intimately connected to the person behind it.

As well as illustrating this very specific conceptualization of what a 'face' is, this fifty-year history of FRT also illustrates the very specific type of 'recognition' that the technology is capable of. In this respect, the term 'facial recognition' is a profoundly misleading misnomer: automated systems do not re*cognize* faces in the sense according to which we typically use this term, precisely because they lack cognitive capacity. As demonstrated in the work of Bledsoe, Sirovich and other pioneers, any match generated by an FRT is probabilistic – in a way quite distinct from what it means for humans to recognize one another. When a person sees an acquaintance from afar, they do not generate a probability score for the match. Nor do they generate a list of possible matches that can be expanded or contracted according to an acceptable level of false positives or negatives. Machines can neither recognize us or know us, they can simply generate a probability that a detected set of parameters align with a stored set, and this probability can never reach 100 per cent certainty. This fact raises some very serious social challenges for any sorting system that relies on fully automated recognition systems. One of the dangers posed by the colloquial use of the term 'facial recognition' is that it sidelines this important distinction, suggesting the possibility of a machine that might actually know or identify someone, rather than simply generating a set of probabilities.

This notion of facial recognition as an abstract mathematical pursuit is also reflected in the relative lack of concern (or even consideration) over the past fifty years for the social and cultural limitations of the technology. One recurring fault line that will feature throughout this book is the problematic entanglement of facial recognition with matters of race and racism. The historical development of FRT just outlined in this chapter in notable for its complete lack of engagement with these issues. For example, when approached from a dehumanized mathematical perspective, it perhaps makes good sense to work with the least 'noisy' and error-prone sets of data. As we have just seen, this tended to lead white middle-aged researchers to seek out datasets populated with pictures of faces fitting the white, middle-aged profile of what they deemed to be 'Mr. Average'. This justification is made repeatedly throughout by the pioneering research teams noted earlier in this chapter – to take two examples:

> The population was deliberately made homogenous to the following extent: all persons were white males, aged between 20 and 50, beardless, without eyeglasses, and had no obvious abnormal features. (Goldstein, Harmon and Lesk. 1971: 749)

> Since our initial goal was to demonstrate feasibility, we endeavoured to create a relatively homogenous population, viz. smooth-skinned Caucasian males. (Sirovich and Kirby 1987: 521)

Even when commercial systems began to notably fail to 'recognize' Black faces in the 2000s, initial responses from industry, media and customers made light of this 'funny' software glitch, usually presuming it to be caused by 'insufficient foreground lighting' (Simon 2009). In some ways, then, this lack of concern reflects the accompanying sense throughout much of its history that facial recognition has been lacking a clearly defined serious purpose or application in mainstream society. Even at the end of the 2010s arguments were still being made that 'it seems that facial recognition is being promoted as a solution for a problem that does not exist' (Wiewiórowski 2019). People twenty years ago can perhaps be forgiven for making light of the limitations of a technology that did not appear to be intended for deployment in any widespread meaningful manner. As shall become clear throughout this book, there is no justification to forgive such oversights in the 2020s.

This lack of clear impetus and purpose is certainly reflected in the main sources of support for the initial development of facial recognition technology. As reflected in the work of Bledsoe through to Pentland and Turk, across most of its history facial recognition research has not been a commercial endeavour, but has instead been sustained by prolonged funding from various US military sources as well as financial support from the likes of the FBI and other security agencies. As with other surveillance and security technologies, the origins of facial recognition lie in the US military–industrial complex of the late Cold War era. As such, FRT development from the 1960s onwards mirrors the ebb and flow of US government funding for many computer technologies and nascent artificial intelligence (AI) – not least the military leadership of science and technology funding during the Cold War period of the 1950s, 1960s and 1970s (Edwards 1996; Leslie 1993), and the subsequent resurgence of funding with the post 9/11 push for 'anti-terror' technologies during the 2000s and 2010s (Noll 2003). As with many areas of computer science, facial recognition has been built on plentiful government funding, sustained political support and integral involvement of actors such as the SRI (an independent spin-off from Stanford University supported by military funding), military contractors such as Bell Labs, and institutions such as MIT that were at the heart of US defence research. This heritage has continued into more recent framings of facial recognition development by the likes of Amazon, Google and Dell in their role as 'a new "military–technology complex" to replace the military–industrial complex of the 20th century' (Alang 2018).

Notwithstanding these military and government connections, a clear sense also emerges throughout this history of facial recognition as something that is often presumed to be relatively neutral. For example, even by 2004, the UK civil liberties group Liberty saw little to take issue with, stating that 'our position on [facial recognition] is neutral. It's another form of identifying and it's no different from traditional photography or fingerprints.' In contrast, the uptake and (mis)use of FRT by law enforcement and security agencies over the past ten years or so gives the lie to the contention that these technologies are merely 'neutral' tools that people can use freely in any ways that they wish. Instead, there is much in this history of FRT to foreground the fact that this is a technology with a distinct set of underpinning values and politics. In the political theorist Langdon Winner's (1986) terms, facial recognition is clearly a technological artefact that has been long designed to have particular social effects. At the same time, facial recognition is clearly a technological artefact that requires specific social conditions and political arrangements to operate – especially with regards to principles of privacy, visibility and individualism. Even the initial tentative uses of facial recognition during the 2000s and 2010s prompt us to think about how FRTs are designed to permit, allow or encourage certain forms of action that are associated with particular power structures and forms of control. We can also think how the idea of facial recognition resonates particularly with certain institutional contexts and institutional politics – for example, being readily adopted in already authoritarian institutions with existing cultures of surveillance, or in spaces where it is believed that more should be 'known' about the people who pass through.

Facial recognition in the 2020s: conditions for mainstream adoption

As we discuss in detail throughout this book, the social, cultural, political and economic conditions of the 2020s are now arguably more conducive than ever to the continued uptake of facial recognition. One recent historical precedent for this has been ongoing repercussions of the generalized sense of risk associated with the authoritarian nationalism that emerged in response to the post-9/11 'War on Terror'. Indeed, directly after the attack on the World Trade Centre, western countries were rife with discussions about the need to deploy facial recognition in airports and at border checkpoints. This was followed by an early instance of high-profile 'security theatre' with widely reported claims that facial recognition had been used to confirm the US military killing of Osama bin Laden in May 2011. In reality, US authorities relied on DNA analysis and testimony from family members to confirm their victim's identity. Nevertheless, if this technology was promoted as playing a conclusive part in bringing down what the *New York Times* described as 'the most hunted man in the world', then clearly it could be used for more mundane domestic purposes.

The deployment of facial recognition technology follows a shift in the surveillance landscape with respect to risk detection and management. The 9/11 attacks in the United States heralded a reconfigured conception of threat assessment. The war on terror envisioned a multiplying array of potential threats. For example, if a surprise attack could come from a civilian airliner, what other potential surprises lay in store? A host of potential vulnerabilities were enumerated after the attack: municipal water reservoirs, port facilities, power plants, and more. The landscape of risk expanded dramatically, and with it the perceived need for increasingly comprehensive surveillance as well as a host of emerging technologies to enable it. DARPA's

Total Information Awareness campaign, inaugurated in the wake of the 9/11 attacks presaged an approach to national intelligence and security that echoed the all-encompassing data collection model of the nascent digital economy and Google's stated mission a couple of years earlier of organizing 'the world's information'. The growth of the internet as a social and commercial medium fed the very forms of risk that the development of digital technology promised to address. It amplified concerns about mediation as a source of deception and uncertainty: more people could access one another directly than ever before, which enhanced some forms of sociality, but also opened up the space for a range of identity theft, fraud, and scams from 'catfishing' to advance-fee 'Nigerian prince' schemes. The prevailing sense around this time prioritized collecting as much information as possible, providing fresh impetus for expanding monitoring and sensing systems in as many dimensions as possible.

The 2020s continues to be a time when these repercussions and concerns reverberate – not least in the normalization of camera surveillance and the monitoring of people's movement. These are times when the imposition of security cameras and other forms of monitors, sensors and tracking devices into our public spaces continues to increase. For example, London is now estimated to accommodate over 500,000 closed-circuit television (CCTV) cameras, whereas China is reported to have a CCTV network exceeding 550 million cameras. Airports, shopping malls, pedestrianized streets and other public spaces continue to be deemed places of potential terrorist risk. While calls to 'defund the police' fade from mainstream discourse, law enforcement agencies continue to make use of surveillance technology provided by tech companies with a financial incentive to trust the police. As Andy Jassy reasoned in a PBS Frontline interview prior to succeeding Jeff Bezos as CEO of Amazon, despite industry moratoriums on police use of FRT, ultimately law enforcement uses of the technology are beyond reproach:

We don't have a large number of police departments
that are using our FRT, and we've never received any
complaints of misuse. Let's see if they somehow abuse the
technology. They haven't done that. To assume they're
going to do it and therefore you shouldn't allow them to
have access to the most sophisticated technology out there
doesn't feel like the right balance to me. (Jassy 2019)

The apparent common sense of having *more* sophisticated
FRT in our lives is reinforced by various other ongoing reconfigurations of society in the 2020s. For example, FRT fits
well with ongoing urban regeneration efforts under the guise
of the 'smart city' – with facial recognition cameras seen to
be ideal ways to generate data-driven insights into flows of
people around urban environments, controlling access, and
generally allowing authorities to track individuals as they
move around crowded public spaces.

Interest in these forms of FRT certainly came to the
fore during the reorganizations of daily life prompted by
the COVID-19 pandemic – not least the mass take-up of
location tracking and technological monitoring of crowds to
ensure the maintenance of social distance, as well as allowing
non-contact forms of access. At the same time, we are now
living in an era where cameras are embedded into the billions
of personal digital devices that people carry around with
them on an almost constant basis (such as smartphones and
laptops), through to domestic appliances and even children's
toys. Accompanying this has been the voluminous production
and sharing of photographic images of faces on the internet –
most notably through social media. As Jason Fox (2018) puts
it, 'cameras a[re] technologies that are increasingly constitutive of our environment.' All told, we now live in times
where we expect – if not encourage – cameras being used to
document our faces.

Perhaps most significantly, FRTs fit with the broader
ongoing rise of artificial intelligence technologies. At
present, the growing use of AI technologies remains a

highly contested topic. On one hand, the IT industry and policy makers continue to make claims about the imminent transformative outcomes of everything from 'industrial revolution 4.0' to 'precision medicine' and 'smart agriculture'. At the same time, there are growing public and regulatory concerns regarding the overreach of technological advances in areas such as automated transport, dataveillance and biometric monitoring. FRT is folded into widespread enthusiasms *and* concerns over the broader ongoing automation and datafication of society, and the entrenchment of 'a Silicon Valley worldview where advances in software and AI are the keys to figuring out almost any issue' (*New York Times* 2020b).

All told, then, the FRT of today is unrecognizable from the initial efforts of Woodrow Wilson Bledsoe and colleagues to cajole a computer into recognizing ten different faces. Now facial recognition technology is an integral element of a wider assemblage of automated vision and what Nora Khan (2019) terms the 'machine eye' – images of people and things being continuously monitored, noticed, labelled, sorted and judged by computerized technology. As just noted, many of us now live in urban environments that are replete with cameras, sensors and other automated technologies of surveillance. This hardware produces a vast and constant stream of photo-graphic images of faces in live video feeds and other forms of real-time 'capture'. These images contribute to rapidly accumulating datasets of facial images – often culled from publicly accessible personal photographs, as well as official databases for licences, passports and other aspects of state administration. These images are recycled and represented in a number of different ways. Oftentimes they are processed only by other technologies, but sometimes they resurface in the course of work, home life, leisure and other moments in our daily routines. Indeed, the faces of 'real' people make up a significant proportion of contemporary digital visual culture. All told, one of the surprising ways in which 1990s' fears over the disembodied, impersonal and anonymous digital age has panned out is that far more emphasis is now being placed on the biological face as a permanent maker of authentic, validated identity. If there was a facelessness to the early internet that provided a sense of anonymity in a world primarily documented in text, the subsequent social media platforms of Web 2.0 placed the face front and centre in a growing range of contexts and applications.

Conclusions

As the next six chapters will demonstrate, FRT needs to be taken very seriously as a social – as well as technical – presence in our lives. In contrast to even a few years ago, it has become a powerful technology. It has become standard for FRT developers to boast levels of well above 99 per cent accuracy for one-to-many matching (that is, picking a face out of a crowd and matching it to an image in a stored database). As a result, FRTs are being developed for all sorts of purposes and places, ranging from law enforcement and the military, to shopping, airports, and social services. Given this range of uses, we need to unpack the intertwined logics that drive the current deployment of this technology – especially the ways in which the wide array of problems that facial recognition now offers to solve often seem to arise from the underlying imperative to collect as much information as possible about individuals to enhance increase efficiency, speed, reach and control.

In addition, it is important to pay attention to the everyday lived experience of coming under the scrutiny of various forms of facial recognition as we go about our daily lives. Even the most narrowly focused of facial recognition systems can result in sustained coverage of the people that fall under its gaze. For instance, a recent trial program of facial recognition cameras installed in one Texas school district reported over 164,000 detections over the course of just one week. This resulted from uploading a modestly sized set of just over 5,000 target student images for the system to search for. One student was reported to have been detected 1,100 times – averaging around 220 times for each day they attended school (Ng 2021). Here, then, we need to consider how the promised benefits of such facial recognition systems (which might well include child safety or organizational efficiency) come with a host of concerns about the fate of privacy and autonomy in an era when everyone can be tracked wherever they go, all the time. These benefits and concerns are not likely to apply equally to all individuals and will clearly differ according to the contexts under which the surveillance takes place.

Given this mix, it is important to engage with the promises and problems that we might associate with the use of facial recognition in a nuanced and balanced manner. At the moment, most popular and policy discussions remain focused primarily on whether FRT is an essentially good or bad thing. Yet, in many ways the most pressing questions to ask are 'How did we come to get this technology?' and 'What do we want to do next?' In addressing these questions, it is important to explore various constituent elements that go to make up facial recognition technology. As Stevens and Keyes (2021) note, 'FRT is not a single technology but an umbrella term for a set of technologies that provide the ability to match an unknown face to a known face.' There is no one version of the technology that we can decide to accept or reject – rather, there is a range of technologies with varying capabilities and applications. It is quite possible that someone who finds the use of facial recognition objectionable when deployed in a shopping centre to track people's interests and behaviour might be fine with using it to verify a signature on an electronic document. Thus we need to consider the various combinations of applications, programmers, hardware manufacturers, marketers, datasets, algorithms, testing standards, legal obligations, institutional purchasers, operators and users that go to constitute what we see from afar as 'facial recognition'.

In the chapters that follow we engage with a broad range of FRT applications and uses in a critical yet balanced manner. This need for balance is important when making sense of such a contested and controversial technology. There is also a practical element to this approach. Even if we were to decide that any use of the technology in any context whatsoever is by definition pernicious, this conclusion would tell us little about how to address the economic imperatives behind its development combined with public support for the use of the technology for some forms of law enforcement, convenience, and efficiency. Given the array of initiatives already in place and the technology under development, it is a crucial time to anticipate the social consequences of the application of facial recognition technology. As we shall see in subsequent chapters, this is technology that is already well integrated into various areas of society. This is not a technology that can be easily banned outright, let alone abolished or un-invented. Anyone looking to argue meaning-fully for the curtailment of FRT needs to engage with the various ways in which this technology now exists, and the strong impetus that many people feel merits its continued development.

Conversely, proponents of FRT (whether they be devel-opers, vendors or purchasers) need to properly engage with the concerns, criticisms and antipathy that is being increas-ingly directed towards this technology. These are important social and political issues that cannot be arrogantly dismissed as the result of people not fully understanding the computer science that drives FRTs. Neither is facial recognition an essentially 'neutral' technology that can be 'fixed' using better data or more socially aware algorithms. Instead, anyone looking to defend the continued spread of FRT into everyday lives needs to be well aware of the political ramifications of doing so. In this spirit, the next six chapters explore how competing meanings of facial recognition have been produced, contested, directed and might eventually stabilize. This approach recognizes the different influences, interests, motivations and experiences of everyone involved in ongoing societal discussions about the technology – be they powerful or peripheral, technically minded or socially concerned. In the following chapter, then, we take time to consider some theories, perspectives and different lines of thought that underpin current understandings of what FRT is, and what it does.

2
Facial Recognition: Underpinning Concepts and Concerns

Introduction

At this point, it is worth taking a closer look at the technological advances and public concerns introduced in chapter 1. In particular, we can consider the various logics and concepts underpinning the integration of facial recognition technology into the activities of contemporary society. There are three distinct areas of thought to consider here. First there are the basic computational logics, ideas and concepts that underpin the technical challenge of 'recognizing' faces from digital images. From this perspective, facial recognition is a complex mathematical problem that has benefited from some neat statistical and computational advances. Here the face is conceived primarily as a data-information object, with any act of 'recognition' or 'identification' more accurately described as an act of statistics-driven pattern matching. Secondly, are the various psychological and physiological theories of the face that have guided some of the recent advances in facial analysis and facial detection. In particular, we consider how computational analysis of the face is seen by some people as a ready means of 'affect detection', as well as of inferring characteristics such as race and gender – thus revitalizing long-standing ideas of physiognomy and other forms of 'reading' human faces.

Finally, we need to begin to get to grips with the various socially focused critical concerns beginning to be levelled against facial recognition. In particular, it is worth considering how the development of facial recognition technology is increasingly bumping up against contemporary theorizations of surveillance. Themes covered in this section include facial recognition as a form of post-panoptic 'monitoring at a distance', as well as issues of all-encompassing algorithmic surveillance. All told, a range of different critical perspectives have long presumed the face to be a particularly revealing object. Face scanning can take place unobtrusively, at a distance, but it is also a deeply intimate and invasive act. This combination requires our sustained consideration.

Fundamental computational concepts and logics

As described in chapter 1, facial recognition essentially involves making measurements of key features from someone's face. These features might include how far their nose protrudes, how their eyes align, or how their chin is dimpled. As few as five carefully chosen facial features can comprise a dataset that is unique to an individual, although the most sophisticated facial recognition systems might measure over one hundred features. These measurements are commonly taken from photographic images but can also be made by sensors that shine light beams onto the face, thus measuring the key facial features without technically photographing the face.

The process of 'recognition' sees these data points from the newly measured face compared with data-points already extracted from existing photographs in order to look for a match. This can lead to two distinct forms of 'facial recognition'. The most straightforward process involves *verification* – addressing the question of whether someone is who they say that they are. This requires a process of 'one-to-one' (1:1) matching. Here the individual's face is scanned and then matched against one existing image of the target person. This 'authentic' image might be already held in a database, such as employee records in a workplace, or from national records of passport photos. In some cases, the image is simply pre-supplied, such as a smartphone owner uploading a photo on the device so they can unlock their phone using their face. This process will confirm whether someone presenting themselves to be Jane Doe is actually Jane Doe or not. This form of authentication allows Jane Doe to unlock her smartphone, access her bank account, or walk through the entry doors at her workplace. If no match is made, then the system simply decides that this is *not* Jane Doe and the process stops.

A second more complicated process is *identification* – addressing the question of who someone is. This requires a process of 'one-to-many' (1:n) matching. Here the matched image comes from existing photographs found in comprehensive (sometimes population-wide) datasets, such as drivers' licences or national ID cards. This process allows the identification of otherwise unknown faces, usually unbeknown to the target individuals involved. Here individuals' faces are compared across a large database of faces until matches are found. This will identify whether we are looking at Jane Doe, John Doe or anyone else in the database.

A third process associated with facial recognition is more accurately referred to as 'facial analysis', given that the target individual is not necessarily being identified. This involves *inference* – i.e. answering the question of what might be known about someone. This might involve inferring demographic characteristics such as likely age, gender and race, or perhaps someone's emotional state or even intentions. Here the data from a scanned face is correlated against measurements that are derived from pre-designated faces with the particular characteristic – for example, 'smiling' or 'depressed'. While the veracity of such calculations remain highly contested, such systems are sold on the basis as being able to provide plausible indications without necessarily identifying the person concerned.

As described in chapter 1, the accuracy of facial verification and facial identification technologies has been improving rapidly, often now reaching claimed levels of 99 per cent and above. Of course, as with all data-driven processes, this still leaves some room for error, which is usually described as taking one of two forms. A false positive involves facial recognition software erroneously judging two images to be of the same individual. A false negative involves failure to match two images that are actually of the same person. Clearly, the consequences of each form of error can be very different depending on the circumstances and rationales behind why the match is being made. False positives can lead, for example, to arrests of innocent people or incorrect risk evaluations that lead to over-aggressive responses on the part of authorities. False negatives can lead to denial of access or other benefits to which people are rightly entitled.

Working to reduce these errors is a fundamental challenge for all facial recognition developers. In ideal circumstances, a facial recognition system will have a database of well-lit, well-posed, high-definition photographs which can be compared with a new image of the face that is similarly well lit, well posed and in high definition. The best-case scenario involves a flat angle, with no face coverings or other intrusions in the images. In this manner, the gold standard for FRTs is often reckoned to be the facial recognition set-up seen in many airports where head-height images from well-lit airport departure gate cameras are compared with similarly posed passport photographs.

One ongoing technical challenge for facial recognition developers is being able to make accurate and reliable matches in less than ideal circumstances. The accuracy of any facial recognition system is understandably compromised by poorly lit images taken from highly placed cameras – situations that result in what are sometimes referred to as 'non-compliant' photos or 'in the wild' images. Another long-standing challenge is partial face identification, when people's faces are obscured by hats, glasses, niqabs, burkas or face masks. A further complication is the challenge of 'liveness detection' – put simply, how the system can be certain that the newly acquired image is of a genuine living person in front of the camera, rather than a high-definition photograph of a face or an impostor wearing a lifelike latex mask. Such challenges might not seem serious for a human observer glancing up and quickly recognizing someone that they know, but can be incredibly difficult to address in computational terms.

The computer science of facial recognition

Next, then, it is worth exploring the basic computational logics, ideas and concepts that underpin FRT as an area of technology research and development. In computer science terms, facial recognition is part of the broader fields of 'computer vision' and 'machine vision' which focus on engineering computers to extract information from images in a similar manner to the human visual system. Computer vision is therefore interested in programming computers to identify objects, perceive distance and motion, recognize patterns and so on. More specifically, much of the technical development of facial recognition is related to the computer vision subfields of 'object detection' and 'object recognition'. In this sense, human faces are just one of thousands of different objects that computers are being trained to detect – from red traffic lights to boxes in a warehouse.

To accomplish this detection and recognition of facial 'objects', facial recognition systems perform four steps. Key concepts here include programming computers to visually detect the specific 'landmark' features that constitute the object class of a 'face' in an image. In any act of facial recognition, object detection principles are used to find the locations of all objects in the image that conform to the main features that programmers consider to constitute a forward-looking profile of a human face. These facial aspects of the image are then segmented from the rest of the image. These facial segments are then converted into grey-level images that are aligned and normalized for lighting, face pose and shirring (head movement). One common approach in face object detection is to use so-called 'genetic algorithms' to detect all possible occurrences of human eyes in the image, often searching for 'valley regions' relating to eyes in the grey-level image. This is then repeated in searches for other 'valleys' related to eyebrows, irises, nostrils and mouth corners. All these searches and checks eventually result in a feature vector of the face being established – a set of statistical data relating to the measurement of these features. The 'fitness' value of each possible face is then calculated by being projected on a number of 'eigenfaces' – the composite images of hundreds of actual faces introduced in chapter 1.

This process only takes microseconds but is underpinned by various complex statistical techniques and theories, most notably the training and development of various algorithms. A range of different algorithms underpins the technical steps just outlined, including algorithms that identify and extract facial features, others that normalize and compress the face images, geometric recognition algorithms that compare distinguishing features, and photometrical algorithms that reduce images to a set of data points. Some FRTs make use of holistic algorithms that attempt to compare full faces, whereas some systems make use of feature-based models that concentrate on comparing a few landmark facial features.

Alongside advances in camera hardware, the rapid development of FRT over the past 20 years or so has stemmed from the development of a number of increasingly sophisticated algorithms. For example, one notable breakthrough involved Paul Viola (then working for Microsoft Research) and Michael J. Jones (then working for Mitsubishi Electric Research Laboratory) developing a face detection algorithm

in 2001 that was 'capable of processing images extremely
rapidly while achieving high detection rates'. The resulting
Viola–Jones algorithm paved the way for real-time facial
detection from video images, and is still in use today. In
essence, the Viola–Jones rapidly scans small rectangular
segments of an image, looking for properties that are deemed
common to all human faces – such as relative locations
of eyes, nose and mouth, or the fact that eye regions are
typically darker than upper cheeks. Despite being limited to
frontal face images, this algorithm underpinned the rise of
real-time FRT during the 2010s.

A key element to the computational development of any
of these algorithms is training them to identify the landmark
features of a face. This requires supplying the algorithm
with a training dataset of pre-labelled images of faces, and
a comparison dataset of non-facial images. Traditionally,
the pre-labelled datasets contain 'ground-truth' labels that
have been manually determined by human coders, thus
allowing the machine to reach human-like decisions. This
training process involves the algorithm 'learning' from this
pre-labelled data, recognizing patterns and setting minimum
thresholds for determining whether a new image should be
similarly labelled. The accuracy of the resulting model can
then be calibrated on a 'testing' dataset comprising various
facial and non-facial images.

Traditionally, this process has required large numbers of
different pre-labelled and cleaned images – an onerous task
for most research teams and developers. For example, the
Viola–Jones algorithm was developed from 4,960 images
featuring facial features (each manually labelled) and a
corresponding set of 9,544 non-facial images. Over the
years, large sets of labelled facial image datasets have been
developed and shared amongst facial recognition developers.
As mentioned in chapter 1, early examples include the FERET
(FacE REcognition Technology) dataset developed from 1993
onwards and funded by US defence and counterdrug agencies,
as well as the MEDS-I and MEDS-II datasets developed for

the FBI. More latterly, large datasets have been compiled from digital images 'scraped' from the internet – for example, the Labelled Faces in the Wild (LFW) dataset, Google's Facial Expression Comparison Dataset, as well as a number of CelebFaces Attributes datasets which also feature various demographic and personality attributes labelled on the basis of what is known publicly about the celebrities whose faces populate the dataset.

These recent datasets comprise millions of images, boosted by the availability of publicly accessible facial images from social media and other online sources. For example, Oxford University's VGG Face2 dataset was released in 2018, compiling 3.31 million images drawn from Google Image search. Another key accelerant to the development of more accurate facial recognition algorithms has been the growing use of 'deep learning' AI – an advanced form of machine learning used to model and develop algorithms using artificial neural networks. Deep-learning techniques are considered by many computer scientists to be especially suited to pattern recognition tasks and are credited by NIST to have led to a 'massive reduction in error rates over the last five years'. In fact, NIST credits deep learning as driving 'a revolution rather than the evolution' of facial recognition during the 2010s. In this sense, facial recognition is one of many areas of technology development that is being driven by general ongoing advancements in AI and automated decision making. As far as many computer scientists are concerned, the capabilities of facial recognition are set to expand and improve at rapid rates through continued advances in AI.

Facial recognition as a computational challenge

These recent advances notwithstanding, facial recognition remains a hugely complex mathematical problem. What a human would immediately perceive as another person's face is quickly reduced to a set of data points, and then subjected to complex computational procedures. As with any complex data process, it is therefore accepted that no facial recognition system will ever be completely free from error. The computational challenge for all facial recognition developers is thus to improve accuracy and reduce errors as far as possible. A good example of this mindset is illustrated by the ways in which computer scientists have set about addressing the recurring technical disparity between the capacity of FRTs to deal with white faces as opposed to non-white faces.

First is the well-reported issue of facial detection technology drawing a blank and simply failing to register the presence of non-white faces at all. There are many aspects of facial detection that make this a complex computational task. In terms of object detection, most facial recognition systems are working from two-dimensional images of human faces that are actually three-dimensional and susceptible to alter considerably in appearance according to lighting, posture and facial expression. In this sense, any propensity to not detect a face is often claimed to be primarily an issue of illumination. Second is the well-recognized propensity for FRTs to misrecognize faces of colour – as evident in the false-positive matches from facial recognition systems that have prompted high-profile arrests of innocent people of colour in the United States over the past ten years or so. As mentioned in chapter 1, the disparities in levels of misrecognition across different skin tones is a long-standing issue, with NIST confirming in December 2019 that 'the majority of facial recognition algorithms continue to exhibit more false positives against people of colour.'

These are not new problems to beset the photographing of faces. Western photo companies have always struggled to cater for darker skin tones – presuming a default of lighter-skinned subjects and only shifting their practices when commercially advantageous. Tellingly, as Ruha Benjamin details in the case of still photography, the primary impetus for change does not usually derive from a concern for racial diversity: 'the photographic industry did not fully take notice until companies that manufactured brown products like chocolate and wooden furniture began complaining that photographs did not depict their goods with enough subtlety, showcasing the varieties of chocolate and of grains in wood' (Benjamin 2019: 105).

That said, since the late 2010s the facial recognition industry has been stung into action as a result of increased public and policy concerns raised over the recurring racial biases in its products. After all, the promise to recognize any face in a crowd is only profitable if there is population-wide coverage. In this sense, computer scientists and technology developers are exploring various technical ways to increase the accuracy of their products. For example, in terms of more reliable facial detection, there is growing interest in 3-D facial recognition systems that can function in low light or completely dark areas. This involves the use of 3-D sensors rather than photographic images – essentially scanning the face with numerous beams of structured light. This results in the production of a set of data points relating to landmark facial features in three-dimensions. These 3-D models can be rotated and aligned to fit with the algorithmic matching process described earlier. Another technical advance is the emerging development of thermal cameras. These abstract renderings of the infrared radiation emitted by faces are seen to overcome the technical problems associated with skin colour and the obtrusion of face coverings, as well as being able to operate at night-time.

Another well-publicized set of technical fixes involves ongoing efforts to ensure that facial recognition algorithms are trained on diverse sets of images – the logic being that machine-learning models developed from datasets comprising mainly white faces will inevitably learn to recognize white faces far better than others. This realignment is certainly understandable, given the provenance of the principal photographic databases that were used in the initial development of FRT. For example, the 1993 FERET dataset was compiled from fifteen different photographic sessions undertaken at US Army facilities and the George Mason University in Virginia – documenting the faces of university staff and students alongside military employees. As Max Kohler (2018) put it, these photographs were 'essentially a time capsule from the campus of George Mason University in the 1990s'. As such, this collection was noted at the time as lacking in diversity. As one report at the same time from FERET researchers acknowledged, 'Some questions were raised about the age, racial, and sexual distribution of the database. However, at this stage of the program, the key issue was algorithm performance on a database of a large number of individuals' (Phillips, Rauss and Der 1996).

Indeed, even in terms of the vague 'ground-truth' labels developed by facial recognition researchers, the most frequently used photographic datasets over the past 30 years have been notably skewed. For example, echoing the nature of celebrity culture, over three-quarters of the CelebFaces Attributes dataset is labelled as aged 45 years or younger. Less understandably, over three-quarters of the Labelled Faces in the Wild (LFW) dataset is categorized 'male', and only 19 per cent labelled as having 'darker' skin colour.

Such gaps and omissions have prompted some notable attempts over the past ten years or so to generate facial datasets that better represent the diversity of faces that an FRT might encounter. This includes IBM's Diversity in Faces dataset – released in 2019 and consisting of one million human facial images taken from the YFCC-100M Creative Commons data set (originally collated by Yahoo! Researchers from Flickr photographs). This collection features a wide range of ethnic and racial groups, what IBM considered to be 'a more balanced distribution and broader coverage'. These photos were all labelled in terms of craniofacial features and skin colour, as well as 'human-labelled predictions of age and gender'. As IBM's marketing trumpeted at the time, 'Have you ever been treated unfairly? How did it make you feel? Probably not too good. Most people generally agree that a fairer world is a better world, and our AI researchers couldn't agree more. That's why we are harnessing the power of science to create AI systems that are more fair and accurate.'

A similar FairFace dataset was released in 2021 by researchers at UCLA. This dataset also used images from the same YFCC-100M Flickr dataset, and consisted of over 108,000 pictures which were 'balanced' across seven different 'race groups' – labelled white, Black, Indian, East Asian, Southeast Asian, Middle Eastern, and Latino (*sic*). When tested with recognizing faces featured in images on Twitter, online newspapers and Web searches, this dataset was found to result in facial recognition systems that were 'substantially more accurate on novel datasets and the accuracy is consistent across race and gender groups'. As the researchers hopefully concluded, 'the novel dataset proposed in this paper will help us discover and mitigate race and gender bias present in computer vision systems such that such systems can be more easily accepted in society' (Kärkkäinen and Joo 2021: 1555).

Addressing and overcoming the issue of bias in training datasets has therefore become a challenge taken up by computer vision and computer detection researchers around the world. For example, at the end of the 2010s, university researchers in China worked to develop improved facial landmark detectors from diverse ethnic group face datasets including Tibetan, Korean and Chinese Uyghur subjects (Wang et al. 2018). Google researchers have even developed alternative measures of skin tones to improve on the six-colour Fitzpatrick Skin Type Scale, which had been relied on by facial recognition developers since the 1970s. As we shall see, there are obvious social problems inherent in all this work. Nevertheless, these efforts are touted by facial recognition developers as leading to 'alternative, more inclusive, measures that could be useful in the development of our products'.

Elsewhere, commercial developers have set about developing various innovative ways to address this issue, such as the production of large 'synthetic data' sets of computer-generated images of faces purporting to represent different racial backgrounds which can be used to augment existing datasets. Increasingly, developers are relying on these synthetic faces and facial expressions to train their algorithms. These are digitally generated faces that look like real people but are simulacra – pure digital fabrications with no authentic real-life person behind the image. Advances in techniques for generating such images make it easy to generate a wide variety of facial types and expressions inexpensively, therefore seen by developers as a way of sidestepping the challenges of ethically sourcing large databases of facial images of real people. In theory, a potentially unlimited number of synthetic images can be rapidly generated for the purposes of training facial recognition algorithms. The drawback, however, is that systems are being trained on simulations that may have their own biases and limitations. Even synthetic images that look realistic to human eyes may differ systematically in important ways from real faces, potentially affecting accuracy rates across populations. Training automated systems to recognize digital fakes is not the same as training them to recognize actual people. Nevertheless, this sense of iterative improvement and innovation drives a belief amongst most computer scientists that, with enough data, any problems identified in the initial implementation of FRT can eventually be remedied.

Facial recognition and the logics of biometric inference

Facial recognition R&D also falls under the aegis of biometrics, extending the computer vision principles of object detection and object recognition into additional logics of object-related inference. In a basic sense, biometrics refers to the use of measurements of the human body to infer information about the person whose body is being measured. Biometric identification has a long history – from centuries-old techniques of fingerprinting and palmprinting through to more recent developments in computer-based iris recognition and DNA identification.

Biometrics is an ambitious area of work, with some of the most interesting areas of current biometrics research actually concerned with finding successors or adjuncts to facial recognition techniques. Other biometric characteristics might eventually prove to be more suitable for identifying individuals from a distance. Some biometric researchers are involved in developing 'gait analysis', identifying an individual from the way that they walk. Others are working on heartbeat analysis, already prompting claims of being able to discern an individual's 'unique cardiac signature' from 200 metres away (Harding 2019). Other areas of biometrics R&D include efforts to algorithmically reconstruct images of an individual's face from audio clips of their voice (Wen, Raj and Singh 2019) or even from DNA traces. Biometrics seeks to extend the range and depth of the insights that might be gleaned from all parts of the human body. Often multi-modal approaches that combine, for example, gait recognition with facial recognition are proposed as techniques for increasing accuracy and reducing bias.

At the same time, biometrics researchers have shown considerable interest in the use of facial analysis techniques to infer personal characteristics and anticipate future behaviours. As Chris Gilliard notes, the promise of knowing *who* a person is from the face seems limited in comparison to the promise of also knowing *what* they are:

Only the most mundane uses of biometrics and facial recognition are concerned with *only* identifying a specific person, matching a name to a face or using a face to unlock a phone. Typically these systems are invested in taking the extra steps of assigning a subject to an identity category in terms of race, ethnicity, gender, sexuality, and matching those categories with guesses about emotions, intentions, relationships, and character. (Gilliard 2018)

Gilliard's use of the term 'guesses' is deliberate, drawing attention to the fact that these are highly contested applications of facial detection and facial recognition technology. Many of these guesses are little more than probabilistic correlations based on existing datasets, and none reach the threshold of 'knowledge' about a particular individual. Nevertheless, such techniques are being developed along a number of different lines, meaning that facial inference is becoming an integral element of the hopes and fears amassing around FRT in the 2020s.

The underpinning mathematical logic of facial inference is one of correlation – looking for patterns of particular facial features that show statistical correlations with other measures. In the same way that algorithms can be trained to detect different facial landmarks, the manual application of 'ground-truth' descriptors to facial datasets can be used to train models to recognize different genders, age ranges or emotions. Alongside the general rise of 'affective computing' (which brings together computer science, cognitive science and psychology), the area of 'facial affect detection' is now fast growing, leading to commercial products that promise to show when students are concentrating, when shop customers are happy, or when street protesters are getting angry and more aggressive. Products such as Faception even promise the capacity to build models that can classify facial features in specific ways – from 'paedophile' and 'terrorist' through to 'professional poker player' or 'bingo player' – without prior knowledge. The tantalizing (but demonstrably false) assumption is that with enough data and computing power, seemingly hidden states and characteristics can be read off the surfaces of people's faces.

This framing of the face as an involuntary revealer of hidden thoughts and intentions is understandably appealing and has led to attempts to infer all manner of characteristics. As Gilliard's observation suggests, perhaps the most obvious characteristics are those of a person's age, gender, racial and ethnic background. Other systems claim to be able to infer mood, attention level and even 'malintent' from facial movements and expressions. Some researchers have even attempted to mine databases of facial images to develop algorithms that can 'read' sexual preference (Kosinski and Wang 2017) or criminal tendencies (Wu and Zhang 2016) from images of people's faces. While the potential uses for these latter applications seem questionable, to say the least, who would not want to have their face analysed in order to make an accurate reckoning of their likely risk of being afflicted by a rare genetic disorder (Gurovich et al. 2019)?

Such tools and techniques are founded on a rediscovery within the affective computing research community of various existing theories of facial features. For example, efforts to link computer-based facial analysis to the detection of emotion have drawn heavily on psychological work such as Paul Ekman's 'Facial Action Coding System' (1973). This was first developed in the 1970s to detect seven basic 'universal emotions', based on the contracted or relaxed state of different facial muscles, combined with eye movements and head movements. Using this facial data, Ekman's theories have long been used by psychologists and other behavioural researchers to calculate emotions such as happiness, surprise, sadness, anger, fear and contempt.

Some critics have been quick to make connections between these high-tech systems and the largely discredited practice of physiognomy – popular in the nineteenth century as a means of assessing character and personality from facial features and facial appearance. While most facial analysis researchers are now keen to distance themselves from past versions of what is largely seen as a discredited pseudoscience, the possibility of computationally analysing thousands of facial images to find statistically significant correlations has prompted a revival of the promise of divining internal truths from surface appearance amongst facial affect detection researchers, especially in terms of personality testing and emotion detection.

These developments serve as ready fodder for theories of evolutionary psychology and associated explanations of links between physical characteristics and behavioural tendencies. Take, for instance, the widely found correlation between large facial width-to-height ratio and 'antisocial' tendencies in males such as threatening behaviour, deception and overall psychopathy. Evolutionary 'explanations' for this include ancestors with wider faces being better protected from fatal blows to the face (and therefore more likely to prevail in physical altercations). This, in turn, is seen to result in an ancestral line more likely to garner influence and power through a capacity to intimidate others (Stirrat, Stulp and Pollet 2012). An alleged association thus gets turned into a wildly speculative account, as is all too often the case with purely correlational findings. Inferential systems that seek to identify criminality or other tendencies and predilections push in the direction of pre-emptive logics that anticipate behaviour based on bodily signals. The goal is not just to record and identify, but to govern behaviour in advance, whether for the purposes of marketing or security. The fantasy of being able to identify criminals' faces, for example, frames criminality in a particular way – not as a social phenomenon but as one of individual essence. As Simon Cole (2009: 303) notes sarcastically: 'Here at last is a promising solution to the problem of crime: hard science that stands in marked contrast to the usual hollow promises of politicians. We need no longer search for difficult social cures for the conditions that breed crime. Instead, we can attack crime at its supposed root cause: the criminals themselves.'

Of course, such work attracts widespread criticism and rebuttal. One meta-review of more than 1,000 different studies found that people will only make the expected 'universal' facial expression associated with their emotional state 20–30 per cent of the time. Many people are well able to maintain emotionless expressions (such as a bluff poker face). Most people are well able to laugh nervously or grimace for comic effect, and many facial expressions are highly culturally specific. As neuroscientist and psychologist Lisa Feldman Barrett (2021) puts it unequivocally, 'detecting facial movements does not equal detecting emotion'. That said, facial affect detection researchers are often keen to point to the statistical associations that their work is based upon. These uses of facial analysis are not usually claimed to be an exact science. Rather, they are presented as offering rough, ballpark guides to likely characteristics – offering outputs that are indicative rather than conclusive, but at least arguably better than chance.

The ease with which a technology that started out as addressing issues of identification slips into social judgements and inferences is, in no small part, testimony to the social significance accorded to the face. As we have seen so far in this chapter, the fact that humans use the face not just as an identity marker but also as a signifying system is easily projected onto machine vision. When people look at one another, they are always reading cues that go far beyond simple identification. Even the briefest of glances at someone's face can give ample evidence of the disposition, mental state and intentions of our interlocutors. Even though this is a function of our own human sense of our internal life (one that machines do not have at all), it is all too easy to project our own practices onto the machines we build. Facial recognition technology mimics aspects of sociality, and it does so with significant social implications. For this reason, it has long been an object of social theoretical research, to which we now turn in these concluding sections.

Facial recognition and the rise of contemporary surveillance

As noted in chapter 1, while facial recognition technology dates back to the 1960s, the model for its current deployment can be located in the importance of ubiquitous, online tracking to the digital economy. The initial expansion of the internet into the commercialized 'open architecture' of the World Wide Web, and then into the 'closed' app-based ecosystem of the smartphone, has enabled a shift in surveillance from what was once an exceptional practice to one that has become virtually universal and multivalent. For transactional purposes the early World Wide Web was largely a memory-less space that could be traversed without leaving recorded tracks. As the *New York Times* (2001) put it, 'at that moment in internet history, every visit to a site was like the first, with no automatic way to record that a visitor had dropped by before.' In the name of convenience and efficiency, the commercial development of the Web over the past 20 years has rested on equipping it with the ability to recognize users as they circulated in virtual space and, eventually, to follow and record their every move, interaction and transaction. The fantastic success of this model has helped inspire the development of ubiquitous and non-transparent monitoring systems that are now also coming to characterize physical space. Here, tracking is experienced as a mostly passive endeavour where we increasingly do not need to show documents to be identified and followed. The result is that the extent of monitoring is invisible to those being tracked.

This model of invisible monitoring is extended further by facial recognition technology. Introna and Wood (2004), for example, describe facial recognition as a 'silent technology' because it can operate at distance without requiring any effort or even awareness on the part of those being monitored and verified. In some contexts (such as unlocking a smartphone or passing through border security), there might still be dedicated actions that need to be taken by the person being identified. However, many other uses of facial recognition technology are effortless and invisible, with an image captured by distant cameras and matched to a database without the target being aware of the process.

All these latter attributes can make the deployment of the technology feel like a form of spying or surveillance, insofar as these are understood to be one way and beyond the control of their targets. Typically, the term 'surveillance' has negative connotations, as suggested by its association with the Orwellian figure of 'Big Brother' government control and oppression, and more recently with economic manipulation and exploitation in the form of 'surveillance capitalism' (Zuboff 2019). However, the influential sociologist of surveillance, David Lyon, points to an aspect of state and social surveillance that tends to get short shrift in the critical literature: 'watching-to-care-for' (Bauman and Lyon 2013: 87). This is surveillance that encompasses 'the intention . . . to protect, understand, care for, ensure entitlement, control, manage or influence individuals or groups' (Lyon 2015: 3). The notion that surveillance can function in the register of care is a familiar one, albeit with overtones of paternalism. We understand, for example, that parents monitor their children in the name of their safety and well-being. Governments track and monitor health trends so as to discern risks and develop strategies for addressing emerging threats. The response to the COVID-19 pandemic, for example, highlighted the role played by public health systems in monitoring the population in order to limit the spread of the virus.

Of course, for those who mistrust the government, such forms of COVID monitoring were framed as invasive, but for the most part people understood the government's legitimate role in safeguarding public health. The surveillance studies scholar James Harding (2019) has argued that surveillance necessarily implies hierarchical and asymmetrical relations that lend themselves to abuse. However, some forms of hierarchy have an important role to play in social organization. Most people want public health agencies to monitor the spread of disease in order to help limit contagion and inform people about protective measures. They also understand that authorities have a legitimate role in developing and deploying processes to limit fraud and other criminal activity. Such claims are not meant to justify the construction of a total surveillance society; rather, they concede the importance of reasonable measures of oversight and control. The real political debate focuses not on whether surveillance and monitoring technologies can be dispensed with, but rather what counts as their 'reasonable' use and what forms of accountability need to be instituted to prevent abuse.

Such questions are reinvigorated by the creeping deployment of facial recognition technology alongside the promise of its alleged benefits and the threat of its potential harms. For example, facial recognition is touted as a useful technology for helping to identify and reunite people (in particular young children) who have been separated from their families by a natural disaster or by warfare. Elsewhere, FRT is heralded as a means to assist in identifying those who may have trouble doing so themselves, as in the case of some Alzheimer's patients. These facial recognition use cases rub shoulders with less caring and humanitarian examples from the realms of policing and security. As a form of monitoring at a distance, then, it is worth approaching facial recognition technology through the lens of surveillance theories, which provide a framework for considering the social issues it raises and its imbrication in social relations of power, control and care. In the following sections, we develop a theoretical understanding of facial recognition technology by considering how different approaches to surveillance inform an understanding of its contemporary context and uses.

Facial recognition as a move beyond panopticism

The rise of the interactive surveillance economy – and the resulting backlash associated with critique of so-called 'surveillance capitalism' – has catapulted a formerly obscure historical term, that of the 'panopticon', into the mainstream. Media commentators have described the rise of facial recognition as creating 'a twenty-first-century panopticon' (*Economist* 2018) and a key element of the increasingly comprehensive forms of data collection associated with the online economy (Karp, cited in Steinberger 2020). In everyday parlance, the term 'panopticon' invokes its Greek roots, referring to an all-seeing apparatus that can monitor people throughout the course of their daily lives. However, this usage does not do justice to the historical origin of this particular use of the term, which derives from the plan of nineteenth-century utilitarian philosopher Jeremy Bentham for efficient management of a prison. Bentham's scheme envisioned an architectural structure that made it possible for one supervisor to monitor an entire prison by creating a central tower with a one-way viewing system into all the surrounding cells. Crucially, the point of Bentham's design was to minimize the cost of running the prison by reducing the need to monitor all inmates all the time. This is the paradox of the panopticon – an architectural model for surveillance that might, at the limit, render its exercise superfluous. Indeed, Bentham's desired result was to create a population that, not knowing whether they were being watched at any given moment, would have to behave as if they were being watched all the time.

Facial recognition technology is the diametric opposite of Bentham's description of panopticism. Facial recognition envisions the perfection of surveillance not by rendering it superfluous but rather by drawing on the agency of technology to make it ubiquitous. As surveillance scholar Mitchell Gray (2003) puts it, an urban space permeated with facial recognition systems inverts the logic of the panopticon. As Foucault observed (2007[1975]), in Bentham's model 'it is at once too much and too little that the prisoner should be constantly observed by an inspector.' As long as the prisoner is conscious of being watched (and adjusts their behaviour accordingly), they do not need to be watched by an inspector. For the model of surveillance ushered in by always-on networks of facial recognition cameras, the opposite is true – the panopticon is at once 'too much and not enough'. As long as people are being watched all the time, they do not necessarily need to be aware of it. Instead, the more uninhibited people are in their behaviour, the more accurate the surveillance apparatus will presumably be in assessing the risk (or opportunity) they pose and responding to it.

At stake in these two versions of 'all-seeing' apparatuses is a differing conception of the monitored subject. The panopticon envisions a disciplinable utilitarian subject – one who calculates the risk of being detected and adjusts their actions accordingly. The model of technologically facilitated real-time monitoring, by contrast, incorporates the prospect of undisciplinable subjects, for whom the threat of surveillance is non-operative. If the panopticon relied on the spectacle of surveillance in the form of the visible tower commanding the prison's central yard (a more ominous equivalent of today's 'Smile, you're on camera' signs in retail outlets), contemporary monitoring systems are often, by contrast, surreptitious and invisible. It is impossible to tell by looking, for example, whether a camera is equipped with facial recognition capability, reinforcing Introna and Wood's description of a 'silent' technology that is 'entirely passive in its operation'. In other words, people do not have to take any particular action to initiate surveillance – it can take place without their knowledge or consent.

Facial recognition and environmentality

As a 'silent technology', facial recognition is also an environmental one that can fade into our surroundings, combining ubiquity with invisibility. In contrast to the panoptic model, then, the intervention of FRT is both actual and targeted. The panopticon is a homogenizing technology that imposes uniform disciplinary norms on the target group, whether these be students, soldiers, prisoners or shoppers. Post-panoptic monitoring enabled by automated systems such as facial recognition enables targeted intervention at scale. This means that crowds can be disaggregated, with individuals pulled out or redirected thanks to modulation of the spaces through which they move. Facial recognition fits this model neatly.

For example, as we shall see in chapter 4, casinos and sports arenas are making use of facial recognition technology to sort crowds at the entrance, picking out VIPs *and* potential troublemakers. Similarly, in response to the COVID-19 pandemic, some airports installed symptom-tracking cameras that would send photos of people with high body temperature readings to roving officers who could pull them out of the crowd for isolation and testing.

This mode of automated recognition goes hand in hand with other technologies of targeting and individualization such as drones, acoustic targeting (the ability to send audio messages to particular individuals in a crowd) and augmented reality. One consequence, as Celis (2020: 307) puts it, is 'that, unlike previous forms of facial representation such as portrait painting and portrait photography, the face in the age of algorithmic recognition is not a matter of individuality and subjectivity but a matter of pre- and supra-personal probabilistic calculations'.

The goal with contemporary forms of FRT is not to recognize an individual, in the full sense of comprehension or concern, but to sort individuals at a granular level for the purposes of intervention and governance. As Rouvroy and Berns (2013: 13) argue, the result is a form of personalization characterized more by 'a hyper-segmentation and hyper-plasticity of commercial offers than comprehensive consideration of the needs and desires specific to each person'. Responding to individuals at scale necessarily tends towards automation as a means of meeting the challenge of individualizing mass response in real time. The environment comes to act not just as sensor, but also as agent – automatically triggering customized responses that might constitute a restraint or opportunity.

The later work of Michel Foucault on environmentality therefore provides a relevant update to the disciplinary model of the panopticon that presages the prospect of a physical environment that can 'recognize' and respond to individuals. Whereas disciplinary power relies on the internalization of governing imperatives (including the rules of 'proper' behaviour) by the subjects of surveillance, an alternative modality of power shapes people's behaviour by intervening in what Foucault calls the 'milieu'. He describes the deployment of an 'environmental technology' which, rather than acting directly on subjects, focuses on the context in which they act. In contemporary parlance, we might describe this as a form of 'nudge' theory – controlling the activity of shoppers, for example, by reconfiguring a shop's physical layout. While Foucault was not writing about the automated reconfiguration of the environment, this notion of environmentality anticipates the ways in which such systems might be used as a form of social control or governance, as in the case of a stadium that uses automated doors and turnstiles to sort VIPs from regular customers.

Facial recognition as a form of algorithmic surveillance

While it is possible for facial recognition to operate according to panoptic logic (by disciplining subjects' behaviour), the technology lends itself to surreptitious uses that depend on supplementary forms of direct action and intervention. This tendency was illustrated in the early use of the facial recognition watchlist at the 2001 Super Bowl in Tampa, Florida. Indeed, the link between external intervention and automated surveillance is a recurring theme in the deployment of facial recognition technology. Traditional CCTV surveillance is faulted by the purveyors of 'smart' technology for simply recording crime as it happens. At best, a CCTV camera can provide after-the-fact evidence, rather than deterring crime or stopping it in its tracks. By contrast, it is claimed that facial analysis cameras can make inferences about what is about to happen and respond by triggering automated forms of response – sounding an alarm, locking down a building, perhaps even intervening physically in real time.

Some systems, for example, claim to be able to detect 'malintent' (the intention to commit a crime) or, similarly, to identify people's moods in order to provide more relevant and effective advertisements (*Guardian* 2019; Swanlund and Shuurman 2018). As mentioned earlier in this chapter, other systems claim to be able to infer everything from attentiveness, mood and intention to trustworthiness, sexuality and even criminality.

Given the role of the face as a primary focus for interpersonal communication, it comes as no surprise that facial recognition would lend itself to such uses. This social function of the face is combined with the interventionist logistics of automated, ubiquitous surveillance, with its imperative not just to watch but also to act. In this respect, facial recognition technology is a subset of what has been more generally termed 'algorithmic surveillance' – monitoring technology that, as Introna and Wood (2004: 180) put it, 'make[s] use of computer systems to provide more than the raw data observed'. A video camera takes a picture, but an algorithmic system adds additional steps, such as matching the image with a database to confirm an ID or reading the target's expression in order to anticipate a response or action. Inferential and operational forms of facial recognition therefore make some type of automated judgement or categorization ('This person is who they say they are' or 'This person is a potential risk'). In turn, this can result in an action: a door is opened, an alarm is triggered, a targeted advertisement is delivered.

Of course, not all facial recognition systems are networked – there many stand-alone '1:n' uses, such as protecting the security of smartphones. However, when facial recognition systems are networked they enable the kind of tracking we have come to associate with dystopian forms of 'total' surveillance. The highly publicized example of China's social credit system, for example, allegedly brings facial recognition systems together with other types of data collection to provide an increasingly comprehensive record of citizens' activities (Curran and Smart 2021). Such a system exhibits traits of both disciplinary panopticism *and* the previously described extra-disciplinary pre-emption. In this respect, such systems combine observation and statistical inference to sort individuals according to what David Lyon (2002) has described as the 'phenetic fix', which places 'people in new social classes of income, attributes, habits, preferences, or offences, in order to influence, manage, or control them'.

Networked facial recognition technology also makes it possible to reconstitute individual time–space paths, enabling both backward and forward tracking. An individual might first be located and recognized at a particular moment. This then allows their past movements to be recalled, and then perhaps even their subsequent movements might even be inferred. Thus FRT enables more granular and less 'punctual' surveillance than 'dumb' CCTV cameras, which are typically used to scan isolated points in time to collect information about specific events. Delivery drivers for Amazon, for example, are submitted to facial recognition ID verification coupled with geo-tracking to trace their movement and progress while out on a delivery run. Whereas in pre-FRT times, the movements of people through the streets might have fallen below the 'threshold at which visibility begins' (de Certeau 1984), the development of facial recognition technology promises to provide new forms of legibility and transparency.

FRT as part of surveillant assemblages

The combination of facial detection, facial identification and facial analysis in emerging deployments of FRT exhibits what theorists have described as the characteristics of a surveillant assemblage. In short, this describes 'the desire to bring [surveillance] systems together, to combine practices and technologies and integrate them into a larger whole . . . with such combinations providing for exponential increases in the degree of surveillance capacity' (Haggerty and Ericson 2000: 610). Various versions of combined surveillance are being promoted as a possible response to concerns about the accuracy of facial recognition systems. As mentioned previously, biometrics researchers are working to develop 'whole-body biometric identification' that combines multiple data sources including, 'face, gait and body type – to improve identification and verification at long ranges and steep angles' (Boyd 2020). Elsewhere, researchers are working to superimpose expression-detection algorithms onto facial recognition images to draw inferences about mood and real-time response to everything from ads to job interview questions.

In the emerging era of biometrics, any analysis of a specific technology needs to be situated within the wider assemblage of which they form a part. In the case of FRT, then, this assemblage will include the sensor arrays – such as cameras, microphones, laser sensor, and so on. It will also include the networks that carry and share this information; the systems that store and analyse them; and the mechanisms that convey a response, whether this be a targeted advertisement or arrest warrant. The face will have an important part to play in this assemblage, given its role in many cultures as both the most visually available body part and the one that already serves as an important social interface. Seen along these lines, then, one socially focused response to concerns about the accuracy of facial recognition technology – concerns which have been used as justification for bans and moratoria on its use – is likely to be the continued development of multi-modal assemblages. This might take the form of adding gait patterns and cardiac signatures to FRT to help increase accuracy across different populations. Predictably, in surveillance contexts, the more common response to malfunctioning systems is not to pull back from deploying surveillance technology but to deploy *more* surveillance technology. These are tensions that we shall continue to discuss across the book.

Conclusions

Certainly, then, there are a number of issues, tensions and questions that come to the fore when these different perspectives converge. For example, one underpinning tension relates to seeing the face as part of a person, in contrast to the face as a data point. Much of the impetus behind the technical development and deployment of facial recognition in society undoubtedly reflects what Judy Wajcman (2019) describes as an 'engineering' mindset that conceives social systems (and the people that live within them) as reducible to a series of key variables. Thus a key issue for social scientists to come to terms with is what the object of FRT is understood to be. In the words of Rouvroy and Berns (2013: xxviii), when deployed at a mass scale, it seems that facial recognition is 'interested in neither the subject nor individuals. All that counts are relations between data, which are merely infra-individual fragments, partial and impersonal reflections of daily existences that data-mining makes it possible to correlate at a supra-individual level.'

A key question, therefore, is what might be lost in the ways in which FRT reduces an individual to a databased representation of their face, and in turn treats this data as proxy for other characteristics. Indeed, as Offert and Bell (2020) argue, computer vision systems do not 'see' faces (or even pictures of faces) in any way comparable to the way that humans see faces. The adjusted and normalized images that facial recognition systems construct contain no information of use to a human observer – these are 'utterly uninterpretable' abstract images that favour shapes over texture, mathematical patterns over human perception. This different way of seeing raises concerns over what Offart and Bell describe as 'perceptual bias'. Reducing a face to a set of data points which are then compared to other data points in an almost endless recursive loop is a computational sophisticated task but also a socially empty exercise.

On the other hand, it is important for those approaching facial recognition from a computer science and data-driven perspective to consider how their 'engineering' logics might be perceived in social and societal terms. This is apparent in the ways in which the prospect of false-positive or false-negative 'errors' are dealt with – i.e. as inevitable statistical occurrences, as contrasted with potentially life-changing breakdowns of a crucial social process for the individuals concerned. This is also apparent in the thresholds for detection and inference. Is a statistically significant correlation between facial data and a crude psychological measure sufficient reason to label a person angry, depressed or motivated? Again, depending on the context in which this information is presented, the outcome of this statistical exercise might have serious consequences for the human being that is implicated as a key part of the equation.

3

Mapping the Facial Recognition Landscape

Introduction

The facial recognition boom of the past ten years or so has been an increasingly commercially driven affair, propelled by various elements of the IT industry. These elements range from AI developers to camera manufacturers, from the largest Big Tech corporations to one-person start-ups operating out of a garage. As with many areas of digital innovation, these commercial activities have benefited greatly from state and government support – most obviously in the form of the substantial funding from defence and security agencies outlined in chapter 1, but also in terms of technical oversight and support. From a US perspective, at least, FRT is a modern-day instance of the 'industrial–military complex', driven by technologists and angel investors, alongside five-star generals, university researchers and blue-chip Fortune 100 firms. At the same time, however, we also have to consider the rapidly increasing production of FRT elsewhere around the world. As we shall see in this chapter, facial recognition is currently the focus of a global scramble to innovate and profit from what many people in the IT industry anticipate will be a defining technology of our times.

This diversity of interests reflects the idea developed in chapter 2 that 'facial recognition' is not a single neat product or process, but rather a broad assemblage of technologies that support the capacity of computers to match a picture of a face with another picture of the same face. Beyond this general definition lies a multitude of different iterations of facial-related computing. If anything, facial recognition is perhaps best understood as a constantly evolving 'umbrella term' (Stevens and Keyes 2021) that covers the activities, agendas and interests of a broad range of different actors and various sociotechnical precedents. There is no distinct 'facial recognition industry' or 'facial recognition community' to speak of. Rather the development of facial recognition is entwined with the commercial fields of computer vision and AI, as well as what is often referred to as the 'biometrics' and 'security' industries. Alongside these commercial fields are various government interests, agencies and departments – ranging from defence to border security, law enforcement to information privacy.

In this chapter, we consider the scope of these actors and their activities – tracing out connections to government sponsorship and support, the influence of Big Tech Silicon Valley actors and the rise of specialist firms from East Asia, Europe and beyond. All these different entities are central to any critical discussion of the recent rise of FRT, let alone for making sense of its possible future development. Indeed, any prospect of the future regulation or reinvention of FRT depends on the agendas of these commercial actors as much as the states, governments and jurisdictions overseeing the regions where their products are used. While the activities of government agencies and the business machinations of the IT industry might not seem like the most interesting aspects of FRT to detail and examine, everything covered in this chapter is integral to making sense of how FRT has come to be the way that it is . . . and how it might develop in the near future.

Government involvement in facial recognition

As illustrated in chapters 1 and 2, the US government has
been a constant driving force in the history of this technology.
The development of FRT in the United States from Woody
Bledsoe onwards has benefited from the official funding *and*
clandestine support of US military and security agencies.
FRT is not unique in this regard. Indeed, many aspects of the
digital landscape have close connections to the US military–
industrial complex – from the late 1960s origins of the
internet from the ARPANET project to the origins of current
consumer GPS products in military development of satellite
navigation. Facial recognition continues this intimate association between government interests and digital innovation
in a number of ways – not least the pivotal role that the
US National Institute of Standards and Technology (NIST)
continues to play in encouraging and enforcing facial recognition standards.

NIST was initially founded in 1901 as the US National
Bureau of Standards, given responsibility for the regulation
of weights and measures, as well as for operating as the
nation's physical laboratory. Amongst its many responsibilities, this is the part of US government tasked with taking
a lead in metrology – the scientific study of measurement and
establishing common understandings of units. Over time, the
Bureau has assumed responsibility for establishing quality
standards in everything from missiles to the first computers.
Since the 1980s, NIST has assumed the task of overseeing the
calibration of software and emerging technologies, including
computer vision and biometric algorithms.

Given its remit for promoting US innovation and industrial competitiveness, NIST has taken a leading role since
the 1990s in regulating and encouraging the development
of FRTs. A key part of this work is conducting evaluations
of new facial recognition products to measure their 'core
algorithmic capability' and gauge the accuracy, reliability

and sensitivity of their outputs. NIST has held various Face Recognition Grand Challenges, where facial recognition developers around the world compete to solve pressing research problems. Perhaps most prominent is NIST's Face Recognition Vendor Testing Program, established in 2000 to assess the capabilities of new facial recognition algorithms. This involves companies, developers and academics submitting newly developed algorithms to NIST who then evaluate and pass judgement on the products' performance. The numbers of facial recognition algorithms submitted to the vendor-testing program have grown from 16 organizations in the 2013 round to the evaluation of 189 face recognition algorithms from 99 developers in 2019. Given its position as an international arbiter of FRT development, NIST also takes on a leading role in establishing the development of various consensus standards that are recognized around the world to benchmark the effectiveness of newly developed systems. In short, many people still adhere to the idea that any FRT is only as good as NIST says it is.

Alongside NIST, a number of other US agencies also have long histories of actively promoting FRT development. These include various intelligence and 'counterdrug' agencies, homeland security and border agencies, various branches of the military, and the National Institute of Justice. Similarly, facial recognition development elsewhere around the world is also often overseen by government agencies in conjunction with their national corporate leaders. In Australia, for example, the Attorney General's Department leads the development of a National Facial Biometric Matching Capability program. On the other side of the world, the French government is establishing an agency and legislative framework to conduct experimental tests of facial recognition systems in public places that will then inform a national regulatory framework.

That said, in comparison to the 1990s and 2000s, these government agencies now play a supporting (rather than leading) role in the continued development of FRT – reflecting the practical fact that governments and other public sector

actors lack the expertise and resources to mass-produce
and market high-tech products on their own. The global
boom of FRT over the past ten years or so has been driven
by private sector and IT industry interests. This has seen
governments around the world work hard to encourage and
stimulate national facial recognition industries. Perhaps the
starkest example of government cooperation with corporate
facial recognition development is Chinese support for the
country's major facial recognition companies. Facial recognition products are an integral component of the Chinese
government's Belt and Road Initiative (BRI) – the major
infrastructure development strategy launched at the
beginning of the 2010s to support Chinese government
strategic investment in various countries around the world.
The BRI has therefore supported Chinese companies such as
Huawei to supply facial recognition products to a wide range
of countries, with sales sometimes underpinned by soft loans
from Chinese banks to encourage poorer governments such
as Algeria, Uganda and Kenya to take the leap to invest in
facial recognition systems.

Of course, government support for FRT is not driven simply
by altruism, national pride or the pursuit of geopolitical
influence. A more direct way in which many governments are
implicated in FRT development is as major direct consumers
of the technology. One particularly keen area of state
purchasing of facial recognition relates to the increased
digitization of police and law enforcement agencies around
the world. As we shall see in chapter 5, police adoption of
FRT now takes various forms – from identifying suspects
to detecting people attempting to use stolen passports,
driving licences or other forms of identity theft. FRT is also
seen as a practical solution to accelerate the analysis of the
mass volumes of digital videos and photographs that police
authorities now receive from eyewitnesses and bystanders in
the aftermath of incidents. In addition, FRT has also been
eagerly taken up by other government agencies tasked with
authenticating identities – most obviously in the form of

identity checks at borders but also in terms of social welfare payments, vehicle licensing and access to other government services where ID is required. Crucially, government interest in FRT has diversified in the form of large-scale urban programs – such as smart cities and smart transportation – supporting everything from the idea of ticketless public transport systems through to reckoning the composition of crowds in public spaces. Given their interest in quickly and accurately determining who people are, FRT is fast becoming a key element of how government bureaucracies and administrations now operate, and of where governments now direct their spending.

Commercial IT industry involvement in facial recognition

As with any area of modern IT, there are many constituent parts to the development, manufacture and sale of facial recognition, involving an array of different elements of the IT industry. The most obvious element of this is the software aspect of facial recognition, not least companies involved in the development of the AI software and algorithms that perform the act of 2-D and 3-D facial recognition. Yet these efforts would be of little consequence without the camera developers and suppliers leading the development of camera hardware – from bespoke hi-res, multidirectional 3-D cameras through to the mini-cameras that are now standard features in smartphones and other digital devices. No less important than the cameras is the infrastructure to capture and interpret the data. One important recent advance here is the boom in companies developing 'edge computing' to support facial recognition analysis – where information processing of data from smart cameras can take place on the spot on smaller servers or even within devices at the 'edge' of the internet, rather than already overloaded core parts of the network. Also key are the software developers and vendors who develop applications and software that make some use of facial recognition capability. Often these are smaller companies with little knowledge of the AI behind their products per se, but nevertheless plug in facial recognition capabilities to their software. Just as modern FRT involves many different elements of government and state support, this is technology that also encompasses an array of commercial interests and industries.

Big Tech involvement in facial recognition

Many readers in western countries might be familiar with the facial recognition efforts of the multinational Big Tech corporations often lumped together under the banner of the 'big five' or GAFAM (Google, Amazon, Facebook, Apple, Microsoft). Indeed, digital technology consumers are likely to have actual experience of engaging with FRTs as developed by brands such as Facebook and Apple. Apple, for example, developed the Face ID technology that allowed them to market the 2017 iPhone X with the promise of 'Your Face is Your Password'. Apple's use of facial recognition to unlock phones and authenticate payments depends on a complex set of technologies – including TrueDepth sensors, cameras and an infrared projector that beams around 30,000 dots onto the user's face to create a detailed 3-D facial map. This data is used to authenticate a one-to-one match as well as to track changes in the owner's appearance over time. Apple also developed various neural networks, bespoke neural chips and software – all for a feature of the phone that most smartphone users now pay scant attention to. Indeed, device unlocking looks set to be one of the most ubiquitous 'active use' applications of facial recognition over the next decade, with over 1.3 billion smartphones expected to feature software-based facial recognition by 2024 (Juniper Research 2020).

Facial recognition has also long been a background component of many large social media platforms. For example,

Facebook was an early developer of facial algorithms to allow their platform to suggest possible matched tagged photographs and videos. Up until 2021, Facebook users had the option to allow the platform to create a face template which could then check for any other photos, videos and images in which they might appear and want to be tagged in. While most users will have given little thought to the process, Facebook's capacity to ask you 'Who is in this photo?' relied on a complex process of facial pattern matching. In contrast to public disquiet over police forces running bystander photographs through facial recognition databases, many Facebook users were subject to this process on a regular basis as the platform attempted to enhance the intimacy and enjoyment of its service.

Perhaps the most prominent way that the development of FRT is being led by these Big Tech interests is through the provision of facial recognition platforms by companies such as Amazon, Google and Microsoft on a 'software as a service' basis – in other words, facial recognition platforms that are centrally hosted and can be integrated into other systems and applications by software developers. This means that relatively powerful facial recognition capabilities can be added to all sorts of existing and new software applications. For example, Amazon's Rekognition and Microsoft's Azure Face software now underpins many of the FRTs that most people come across in their everyday lives. The most widely used of these is perhaps Rekognition. This allows individual software developers to make ready use of powerful pre-trained algorithms – for example, different algorithms trained to infer age, gender and emotions from a photo, recognize celebrity faces, or track the appearance of one specific face all the way through a video. Alternatively, developers can use Rekognition to train their own algorithms on a customized set of faces, perhaps to recognize a small group of people or to find similar-looking faces in a database.

Most Big Tech firms – such as Google, IBM and Cisco – have at one time or another been involved in the development of face-related products, applications and APIs (application programming interfaces) which can be picked up and used by third parties. At the same time, most of these firms engage in large-scale bespoke work for governments, businesses and other organizations. This aspect of work hit the headlines in 2019 when Google workers protested over the company's work on object recognition and video analytics for the Pentagon's Project Maven program. Despite some high-profile pull-backs, this aspect of the commercial facial recognition industry continues apace. All of these GAFAM corporations are in the business of organizing and collecting data, and in this sense faces have become another form of data. Given their dominant rule in the information technology industry, GAFAM interests have played key roles over the past decade in extending the use of FRT throughout law enforcement, military and private security domains around the world. Whether unlocking a smartphone or targeting a remote missile strike, FRTs are being produced and sold by the largest tech corporations for a range of ordinary and extraordinary automations of everyday life. FRTs are becoming a commonplace multi-purpose information processing technology that many industry actors expect will become more ubiquitous than barcode scanners.

Specialist facial recognition companies

While familiar to most readers, these multinational Big Tech corporations are not necessarily at the absolute cutting edge of facial recognition applications. Instead, many instances of innovation in the technology are led by less familiar companies and firms. For example, development of FaceID for the iPhone X relied on technology obtained from Apple buying out a specialist Israeli start-up in 2013 that had developed 3-D sensing technology for computer games consoles. As is often the case with commercial IT 'breakthroughs', this is technology that originates from the efforts of much smaller and less-celebrated specialist designers and developers.

That said, one of the long-standing market leaders in FRT is the Japanese multinational company NEC. Founded in 1898 as an electric and telephone company, NEC has worked on facial recognition development since 1989 – building on its previous work on character and pattern recognition. NEC's NeoFace system was introduced in 2009 and is still widely used and highly regarded for its speed and accuracy. Various iterations of NeoFace underpinned many marquee implementations of facial recognition during the 2010s – including the high-profile trials of FRT at New York's JFK Airport, various Olympic Games and other international sporting events. The latest iteration of the Neoface Watch real-time monitoring system is now used in around 60 countries, with the company boasting over 100 million enrolments and millions of daily transactions.

Other prominent facial recognition developers include specialist companies such as FaceFirst, Ayonix Face Technologies and IDEMIA. All these companies offer similar software development packages that allow other developers to build in facial recognition and facial detection services into their own software and applications. Specific variations of these algorithms are designed for different markets, from retail customer engagement through to law enforcement. These companies are supported by hardware developers that design sophisticated camera, scanning and detection devices. All told, the implementation of any FRT will involve software, hardware and services from a variety of commercial providers, developers and producers. Facial recognition is a complex combination of technologies, and consequently involves a web of different interests and responsibilities.

Aside from these US, European and Japanese interests, facial recognition technologies continue to be a key area of development for a number of leading Chinese firms. While some of these firms cater primarily to domestic markets, perhaps the most internationally familiar of these are companies such as Huawei, Hikvision, Dahua and ZTE. The Chinese tech giant Huawei is perhaps the most globally recognized name – known to consumers as one the world's leading smartphone producers, while also regularly making western news headlines as the focus of US government accusations of cybersecurity violations and undue influence of the Chinese state. As one of the world's leading IT companies, Huawei is involved in a broad range of facial-related developments. Most notably, the company spent much time developing its big data FusionInsight software platform to process facial recognition from real-time video streams. Yet Huawei's interest in FRT is expanding. For example, the firm is also a leading player in developing the commercial roll-out of agriculture facial recognition, such as monitoring and recognizing individual animals amongst the herds kept in China's vast pig farms.

Alongside these large technology corporations, China is home to a thriving domestic facial recognition industry, with hundreds of smaller firms developing technology for the region, some of which is then exported around the world. For example, MEGVII's Face++ division is developing an array of facial recognition-related technologies, including software development kits that allow facial recognition to be added to smartphone and laptop applications. This includes various 'facial landmark' algorithms that range from standard capabilities (using 106 facial points) to dense capabilities (using up to 1,000 different facial points), as well as a 'face compare' algorithm that allows developers to include simple facial ID and photo-matching capabilities in their applications and software. These technologies sit alongside MEGVII's other 'human body recognition' products – including 'gesture recognition' and 'skeleton detection' systems, as well as 'portrait segmentation' systems that detach bodies from images and superimpose them on different backgrounds. As all these examples suggest, such firms are steadily expanding the possible consumer uses of FRT well beyond the applications traditionally demanded by governments and other organizations. As in the case of many tracking and monitoring technologies, once they show signs of promise for a specified set of uses, the industry seeks out new markets and applications.

Crucially, China is also home to many of the world's leading (and cheapest) producers of high-specification smart cameras and scanning technology. As is the case with most consumer electronics, the south-east Chinese city of Shenzhen is the epicentre of this supply chain – manufacturing everything from the high-resolution 3-D and thermal-sensing camera systems to the cheap mini-cameras that fit into smartphones and other personal devices. Few camera hardware manufacturers are vertically integrated to the point of being able to produce all their product components, instead relying on a variety of third-party component manufacturers. Together, these firms are driving the low-cost integration of facial recognition into everyday personal devices and technology products. Now any local software developer can integrate facial recognition into their design, and any local shopkeeper can purchase an inexpensive camera system to add facial recognition capabilities to their security system. Market forces and the entrepreneurial drive of the IT industry are ensuring that FRT is no longer the sole preserve of well-funded government agencies and rich corporations.

A fragile but functioning ecosystem?

As all these examples illustrate, the development and production of FRT is a sprawling and loosely connected ecosystems of actors, interests and agendas. This includes unlikely combinations of corporate interests and government imperatives, the efforts of large multinational corporations and small self-employed businesses, with the same technologies being sold to defence and domestic consumers. All of this makes FRT a complex market. On the one hand, FRT is the basis of multi-billion-dollar Pentagon contracts. On the other hand, FRT involves selling on plug-in APIs for a couple of hundred dollars. In one instance, FRT is the basis of Apple's sophisticated Face ID scanning feature. In another guise, FRT is being produced by lone hobbyists working in their garages to self-engineer simple applications for their own use.

This confluence of academic expertise, commercial innovation and state finance might appear fragile, yet has worked remarkably well up until now in pushing forward what is an undeniably complex technology. One good example of the collaborative and cooperative nature of the business is the steady development of datasets of photographs required to develop and train facial recognition algorithms. As outlined in chapter 2, a key part of facial recognition development is establishing and refining a computational model on a large dataset of photographs of human faces. This usually involves hundreds of thousands of photographs that are pre-labelled with each subject's age, gender, race and other attributes that the new facial recognition system can be 'trained' to 'recognize'. To date, the continued development of such datasets has been driven by training data being shared amongst research teams and overseen by NIST in its guise of independent arbiter. In many ways, then, this illustrates how much of the progress towards the advanced FRTs that we have today rests on a combination of public sector and private sector efforts. In short, this aspect of FRT development frames the technology as a scientific pursuit with iterative advances resting on the efforts of others, and with a collective interest in developing accurate and technically elegant products.

As outlined in chapter 2, compiling datasets of labelled facial photographs is a traditionally difficult challenge – costly to assemble and store. Until recently, these datasets were very expensive to compile, meaning that only a few initial datasets were widely used and shared to build facial recognition systems over the 1990s to 2010s, such as the US government-funded FERET dataset. That said, the past ten years or so have seen the size and scope of these datasets become enhanced dramatically through the involvement of large commercial technology companies. Now the rise of digital photographs has given rise to much larger datasets comprising images 'scraped' from the internet. Vast datasets are now compiled from images sourced from YouTube, Flickr, Facebook and other public places where people post photos and videos. Some of Google's private facial recognition datasets consist of over 200 million images and 8 million different individuals. Some of these internet-sourced datasets are designed to help developers overcome specific challenges that occur when facial recognition moves beyond carefully posed high-definition facial portraits in well-lit contexts. The fact that large datasets of millions of faces can be generated through what is a largely cooperative and collaborative process could be seen as proof that FRT is an industry that continues to be driven by a convergence of public and private sector values.

The cautionary rales of Clearview and PimEyes

Of course, as some of the concerns raised in chapters 1 and 2 suggest, not all applications of FRT adhere to these laboratory ideals of scientific collaboration and a shared pursuit of progress. In contrast, it is important to also consider instances where this balance of shared interests and mutual oversight can quickly break down in the face of more scrappy technical practices and the more aggressive pursuit of profit. One prominent example of this emerged at the beginning of 2020 and the rise to prominence of Clearview AI – a small start-up company that was served with 'cease and desist' notices from Twitter, YouTube and Facebook for its use of facial images from their platforms. Prior to this, Clearview AI was a relatively unknown commercial app developed to pick out any face from a crowd using publicly available online images. The company was reported to have developed the app to match a photo of someone against a proprietary database of 'more than three billion images that Clearview claimed to have scraped from Facebook, YouTube, Venmo and millions of other websites' (Hill 2020) By the time Clearview's product came to media attention, the app was already in use by 600 law enforcement agencies around the world that had been using it to identify suspects from video clips and smartphone photos. The attraction of this particular product was due largely to its coverage and scale, with Clearview claiming that its facial image database was six times larger than the FBI's.

While Clearview attracted vociferous criticism from a diverse range of representative groups and organizations, the company has continued to operate in the face of numerous legal challenges. In 2021, for example, Canadian privacy and information commissioners jointly proclaimed Clearview to have violated federal and provincial privacy laws. As their final judgement put it, 'Clearview AI's scraping of billions of images of people from across the Internet represented mass surveillance and was a clear violation of the privacy rights of Canadians' (Office of the Privacy Commissioner of Canada 2021).

In response, Clearview simply countered that Canadian privacy laws did not apply to a New York-based company. It also argued that people had made these images publicly available, and more perniciously claimed that, 'given the significant potential benefit of Clearview's services to law enforcement and national security and the fact that significant harm is unlikely to occur for individuals, the balancing of privacy rights and Clearview's business needs favoured the company's entirely appropriate purposes' (Office of the Privacy Commissioner of Canada 2021).

It was also noted that 48 Clearview accounts had actually been purchased by various elements of Canadian law enforcement agencies. At the time of writing, Clearview continues to operate – growing its user base to over 3,000 organizations, achieving a valuation of US$100million, and being named by *Time* magazine as one of the 100 most influential companies of 2021. Indeed, the overwhelming majority of facial images 'in the wild' are collected by social media platforms often without explicit consent for the use of such images for facial recognition applications. Now the terms of service for apps and platforms such as TikTok and Facebook are updated to include consent for the collection of face data. This approach has proven relatively non-controversial – once people are using a platform, they are likely simply to agree to updated terms of service without closely inspecting them or thinking about them in order to continue to participate in their online networks.

Crowd-sourced FRT applications that piggyback on the success of commercial platforms in soliciting face images are beginning to spring up with increasing frequency. For example, CNN reporter Rachel Metz reported in 2021 on PimEyes – another online service that invited users to upload a photo and see what other images of the same face it has scraped from the internet. Uploading a photo of one's own face could lead to all manner of images that you are likely to have forgotten, presumed lost or hoped to be lost. As PimEyes marketing promised, 'Using the latest technologies, artificial intelligence and machine learning, we help you find your pictures on the internet and defend yourself from scammers, identity thieves, or people who use your image illegally' (PimEyes 2022).

Whereas Clearview AI claims to restrict its services to a few thousand carefully chosen customers, PimEyes made its product available to anyone willing to pay. As privacy rights campaigners pointed out, this includes your parents, potential dating partners, prospective employers, co-workers or anyone else curious to learn more about your past. For a personal subscription of US$30 a month (or a business account of US$300), the system allowed unlimited high-resolution searches and provides access to an alert service when new pictures of a particular face are found. Unlike Clearview's scraping of images from Facebook and Twitter, PimEyes also scraped images from company, news media and pornography websites. It claimed to have accessed 900 million faces and scraped over 30 million websites. As a small start-up originating in Poland (later re-registered to a holding address in the Seychelles), PimEyes is not a major player in the FRT industry but illustrates a direction of travel as the technology becomes more widely accessible and easier to be integrated into simple Web services. As Metz concludes, 'PimEyes' decision to make facial-recognition software available to the general public crosses a line that technology companies are typically unwilling to traverse and opens up endless possibilities for how it can be used and abused.'

In crossing these lines, these smaller companies might well be paving the way for the more widespread use of facial recognition technology by potentially making one-to-many identification so widely available that it becomes all but impossible to reverse course.

The recent push for oversight and regulation

Concern over the need for oversight of the FRT industry is not confined to the actions of a few rogue actors. In comparison to the work of Clearview and PimEyes, established Big Tech firms are not necessarily more ethically sensitive in their facial recognition work. This was illustrated by reports in 2019 of contractors working for Google being deployed to Atlanta, Los Angeles, and various college campuses across the United States to offer US$5 Starbuck gift cards to homeless people and college students as payment for collecting 3-D scans of their faces. These contractors were reportedly given instructions to prioritize subjects with dark skin (Fussell 2019). In one sense, this strategy makes good commercial sense – Google understandably wants to improve the face-unlock feature of its Pixel phones, and homeless and college populations might be seen as less concerned than other demographics with issues of biometric data collection. Nevertheless, for a technology that is already felt to be ethically questionable, episodes such as this do little to reassure a sceptical public that FRT is wholly above board and for good.

Episodes such as this lead to an increased sense that FRT merits close oversight, governance and regulation. At the time of writing, perhaps the most influential planned regulatory response is taking shape in the European Union, whose General Data Protection Regulation (GDPR) encapsulates the leadership position it has taken in responding to concerns about the surveillance model of the online economy. Leading European experts, including the European Data Protection Supervisor and the European Data Protection Board, have called for 'a total ban on using AI to automatically recognize people' (Burgess 2021). Indeed, both groups issued a joint statement stating that the deployment of 'remote biometric identification in publicly accessible spaces means the end of anonymity in those places' (Burgess 2021). They also called for a ban on the use of automated technology for making predictions about ethnicity, gender, and political and sexual orientation, thus seeking to tackle what can be described as the 'inferential' use of facial recognition technology.

However, proposed EU regulations fall short of banning biometric monitoring outright. Instead, they identify a limited number of conditions under which the processing of biometric data can be deemed lawful and would require any proposed use to be subject to a Data Protection Impact Assessment. As such, the proposed regulation leaves space for the use of the technology for law enforcement purposes – specified in the proposal as 'the objective of preventing, detecting, or investigating serious crime and terrorism' (European Parliament 2021: 48). Indeed, given the commercial pressures to develop the facial recognition industry (as well as rapidly advancing uses of the technology in other regions of the world), it remains to be seen whether the proposed European regulations will be enacted and, if so, what shape they will take and what their international impact might be. It is highly likely that the European response will stand out in counterpoint to that of the United States, which, while leading in the development of the tech industry, has lagged when it comes to regulation. Similarly, China continues to prioritize investment in AI and facial recognition technology as growth industries.

As the European example illustrates, practical regulation of FRT is a difficult task. In a world in which Big Tech companies operate at a regional or global scale, regulation still operates in a patchwork of local, regional, and multinational jurisdictions. In the United States, for example, at least seven states and two dozen municipalities have enacted some type of ban on facial recognition technology. Nevertheless, these 'bans' remain quite variable, with some limited to police and/or government use of the technology, while others ban all use of facial recognition in public (Smyth 2021). The rationale for these prohibitions tends to combine concerns about intrusion and privacy with critiques of inaccuracy and bias in the technology. The American Civil Liberties Union (ACLU), for example, invoked concerns that women and people of colour would be inaccurately identified by the technology, calling on Amazon to stop selling marketing facial recognition technology to law enforcement (Conger, Fausset and Kovaleski 2019). However, these two stated concerns exist in tension with one another since the implied call for greater accuracy *and* less bias would compound concerns about the fate of privacy and the invasiveness of the technology. The perfection of the technology, in short, would render it maximally invasive.

Government approaches to regulating FRT along these lines remains in their infancy. Other civil society groups are therefore also taking a lead in developing clear understandings of the ways in which democracy and civil rights are threatened by the unfettered use of facial recognition technology. This is the approach adopted by groups like Amnesty International, which, in addition to highlighting the biases in existing facial recognition systems, has emphasized the chilling impact that police use of the technology could have on public protest and political activism (Fussell 2021).

We might add to this the impact that commercial forms of targeting and customization have on the social fabric, which relies not just on individual preferences but on a shared sense of interdependence that is eroded by the online model of hyper-individuation and the custom tailoring of the information environment.

Predictably, industry responses to the threat of legal restrictions have been to propose the alternative of self-regulation. Self-imposed bans and pull-backs of facial recognition projects from the likes of Microsoft, Amazon, IBM and Facebook suggest that the major tech companies are wary of the prospect of negative publicity and reduced consumer confidence, and remain responsive (to some degree) to internal pressure from employees. However, these bans are likely to come under increasing pressure as other smaller companies pave the way for increased demand and the prospect of significant profits. In addition to self-regulation, the IT industry is gearing up for a lobbying battle especially in the United States, where bans at the state and local level have driven industry concerns about the prospect of federal regulation. The US Chamber of Commerce was alarmed enough by calls for regulation that it wrote to Congress in 2019, urging against a moratorium on the use of FRT on grounds of both public safety and the economy. The letter argued, predictably enough, that the route to improving the technology (presumably addressing issues of accuracy and bias) lay through more use of facial recognition, not less: '[W]e are concerned that a moratorium on the use of facial recognition technology would be premature and have unintended consequences not only for innovation, safety, and security but for the continued improvement of the technology's accuracy and effectiveness' (US Chamber of Commerce 2019).

Similarly, the Security Industries Association, a prominent industry trade group, continues to lobby against moratoriums on the use of the technology and features a list of 'facial recognition technology success stories' on its website

(SIA 2021). This group has conducted research indicating that, in the United States, 70 per cent of respondents, 'believe facial recognition is accurate in identifying people of all races and ethnicities' (SIA 2020).

Conclusions

Facial recognition is clearly an area of technology development that is growing in size and stature, as well as attracting more attention from government regulators and state legislators. From a commercial point of view, expectations remain high that this sector of technology development will thrive throughout the 2020s and beyond, regardless of future regulation and restriction in some sectors and certain countries. Government bans and self-imposed industry moratoriums might suggest a growing willingness to curtail future growth, but in reality these are very specific forms of facial recognition use. Restricting police and municipal uses of FRT is one thing, but lucrative markets for facial recognition applications are being identified across all areas of society – from unlocking one's smartphone through to being assessed for health insurance. There are clear differences between one-to-one authentication and one-to-many surveillance applications. Many facial recognition developers and vendors would argue that there are clear differences in the diverse applications that facial recognition can be put to.

Industry predictions remain confident that the technology will continue to find profitable new markets – with forecasted market valuations of US$12 billion by 2026 (Global Market Insights 2021). Hopes remain high for growth in large markets such as China and India, as well as for increased application in areas such as banking, financial services, insurance, health care and retail. More speculatively, perhaps, is the integration of FRT into 'smart home' and 'smart city' environments. All told, most people working in the area of FRT remain optimistic about the short-term and long-term prospects. With these different areas of potential development in mind, the next chapter turns its attention to some of the main areas of FRT development that are considered to be of notable benefit and clear pro-social utility. While some areas of FRT might well merit obvious concerns being raised over diminished civil rights or erosions of democracy, there are plenty of other use cases that might be considered far more benign. So what uses of FRT do many people consider unproblematic . . . if not wholly beneficial?

4

Pro-Social Applications:
Facial Recognition as an
Everyday 'Good'?

Introduction

Despite the scale of the industry and investment outlined in chapter 3, facial recognition is a technology that has still not fully progressed to being deployed on a widespread basis in everyday settings. Until the 2010s, there was simply not sufficient computational power, data-processing speed, and data-storage capacity to support large-scale real-time computer vision. Only now do we have the mass presence of sophisticated cameras throughout our everyday urban environments to support large-scale facial recognition. Crucially, only now are we beginning to see enough varied implementations of facial recognition to give the general public a tangible sense of what this technology is, and what this technology can be used for – what technologists like to refer to as persuasive 'use cases' and 'proofs of concept'.

In this chapter, we consider some of the most ordinary – and arguably most significant – ways that facial technology is beginning to be integrated into our everyday lives. Focusing on these ordinary uses is a deliberate step in developing our critical understanding of facial recognition. As we saw in chapter 3, the facial recognition industry is now designing, developing and selling a diversity of systems and products from unlocking one's smartphone through to nationwide criminal surveillance systems. Many readers will have perhaps made use of (or perhaps been unwittingly 'seen' by) facial recognition technology during the past 24 hours. Yet, as is often the case with emerging technological developments, popular and political discussions of facial recognition still tend to remain polarized along utopian and dystopian lines.

As might be expected, IT companies and vendors are keen to promote the benefits of this technology. Automated identification, for example, could well usher in a new era of frictionless access and customization. We can walk into a store, take what we want and have it all charged to our account by cameras that 'recognize' us. No more need to remember PINs and metro passes or to present ID cards or drivers' licences. Yet facial recognition has fast become a controversial technology, and the subject for much recent push-back. Put bluntly, there are many ways that perpetual automated recognition could spell the end of privacy and, if centralized, usher in new forms of authoritarian control that perpetually sorts, categorizes and ranks us. As such, it is important to take a balanced approach to the enthusiasm and concerns that currently surround this technology. How can we cut through the hyperbole of technology developers, the profit-led promises of vendors and marketers, and the readiness of stores, stadia and airports to implement this technology? How can we contextualize fears and criticisms raised in terms of civil rights and discrimination? The next two chapters explore these competing narratives by focusing first, in chapter 4, on some of the more mundane and pro-social uses of the technology, and then in chapter 5 turning to more alarming uses and applications.

So in this chapter we consider some of the best-case examples of FRT. It approaches automated facial recognition through the lens of convenience and efficiency, care and protection, as an aid to humanitarian work and even as a source of creativity and entertainment. It explores the range of possible uses of facial ID systems, covering everything from mass transit to education, shopping and security to identify and unpack the guiding imperatives of speed, efficiency and control. What can we make of claims being made about the benefits of facial technology in fields ranging from security to finance to shopping? What are the various 'problems' that facial recognition technology promises to solve, and what priorities emerge from this framing? In short, what good might facial recognition do for us?

Facial recognition as a humanitarian tool

One much-lauded application of facial recognition is the use of the technology to assist vulnerable people. This includes the use of FRT by humanitarian agencies working with refugees and other dispersed populations – part of what has been termed 'humanitarian refugee biometrics' (Jacobsen 2019). Here FRT is used in the maintenance of 'smart borders', along with GPS and other biometric technology, to create 'digital ID' for displaced individuals. Elsewhere, FRT is also beginning to be used to identify unknown migrants in refugee camps. While these problems of famine, natural disasters and war have been with us for centuries, there is a concerted push to bolster twenty-first-century humanitarian aid along lines of high-tech efficiency and precision.

All told, FRT has been welcomed by humanitarian agencies as a solution to the key challenge of tracking and regulating the movement of otherwise unidentifiable large groups of people crossing borders. The World Bank (2017) estimates that more than 1.1 billion people around the world lack identification. At the same time, identification is seen to be an integral element of agencies' capacity to provide these people with access to resources and medical and legal support, as well as to reunite otherwise separated family members. Growing interest is therefore being shown in FRT as a means of overcoming this administrative bottleneck, as well as fitting well with humanitarian agencies' existing information infrastructures. Most significantly, humanitarian agencies have a long history of maintaining photographic identification databases for refugee and other displaced populations. For example, the UNHCR (the UN's refugee agency) has access to a variety of databases under its Population Registration and Identity Management Eco-System (PRIMES) program – providing fingerprints, iris data and facial images of millions of displaced people. While humanitarian services have traditionally favoured fingerprint and iris recognition, there is growing belief that facial recognition can simplify registration and identification processes, as well as being less susceptible to fraud and duplication than is the case with the use of fake irises and 'silicon fingers' (UNICEF 2019).

Elsewhere, much is made of the use of facial recognition to identify missing, kidnapped and trafficked people. For example, one early pilot program by authorities in China reported finding nearly 6,500 missing people as a result of scanning the faces of around 200,000 homeless people. Similarly, Indian police have started to periodically attempt to identify missing children who are being exploited as forced child labour, claiming to be able to reunite thousands of children with their families. One concerted effort in 2018 saw New Delhi police using FRT to identify and rescue 2,930 missing children in four days, after attempts to match 45,000 photos of children living in orphanages and foster homes with photos in India's National Tracking System for Missing and Vulnerable Children. Elsewhere, on a focused one-to-one basis, facial recognition is now successfully used by law enforcement agencies around the world to assist in searches for missing and abducted children, as well as missing adults. These logics also extend to the application of facial recognition technology for disaster victim identification, which is seen as a means of providing closure to families and preserving the dignity of the dead person (Khoo and Mahmood 2020).

Perhaps the most extensive crisis-related application of FRT to date was seen in the early 2020s as authorities struggled to respond to the COVID-19 pandemic in countries such as India, Russia and China. FRT played an important role in terms of COVID-19 tracing and social monitoring. For example, during the first year of the pandemic, Moscow authorities quickly made use of the city's network of 189,000 facial recognition cameras to identify citizens who were failing to comply with self-quarantine orders, as well as monitoring the movements of returning travellers who had recently flown in from high-risk countries. Elsewhere, in the Indian state of Pune, people placed into home quarantine during COVID lockdowns were able to self-report their compliance by uploading selfies to an app. Pune's Home Quarantine Tracking System was designed to verify compliant individuals' identity via facial recognition alongside their geolocation. Similar apps were deployed by police forces in other regions that had previously experimented with facial recognition, such as Tamil Nadu's Tiruvallur district. Facial recognition was also deployed in quarantine hospitals and hotels in Dehradun. Systems that had previously been used mainly by police and security agencies were suddenly able to be deployed in the service of public health.

One interesting development amid these rapid COVID deployments of facial recognition technologies was the sharing of open-source code between software developer communities. This included the rush to develop facial recognition algorithms capable of detecting masks (and the absence of masks). Facial recognition systems were reprogrammed by various Chinese developers and companies to flag people who were not complying with regulations to wear face masks and were therefore deemed a health risk. This AI model was made available by companies such as the search engine Baidu and the ride-sharing company DiDi on an open-source basis. These AI models were quickly adapted and implemented by businesses wanting to ensure that employees or customers were conforming, as well as by police authorities in China and India. As Baraniuk (2020) noted at the height of the pandemic, 'COVID-19 is clearly not only creating challenges for the proponents of facial recognition – but potential opportunities as well.'

Facial recognition in public places

Aside from assisting in times of disaster and emergency, FRT is now part of our lives in many more mundane guises – not least in terms of aiding the movement and management of crowds in public places. The most common instance of this during the 2000s and 2010s was the use of facial recognition in and around stadium spaces. The logic of using FRT in spaces that are temporarily converged on by tens of thousands of people is straightforward enough. Contactless turnstiles can allow large crowds to enter without having to scan a ticket. Thereafter, facial recognition cameras can quicken crowd flow by directing ticket holders to their designated areas – discretely filtering off VIP spectators from those in the bleachers (Hutchins and Andrejevic 2021). Seventeen years after the Superbowl XXXV demonstration in Florida, the 2018 FIFA World Cup in Russia made use of around 500 facial recognition cameras in and around tournament stadia. Organizers claimed to have identified about 100 individuals who were barred from attending matches and to have gathered useful analytics on crowd size, gender and age composition. Shopping malls and large public spaces have also begun to make similar use of facial detection for crowd counting and other analytics, gaining detailed insights into how their spaces are used in order to inform future planning. Elsewhere, large visitor attractions are beginning to make use of FRT for queue monitoring – for example, identifying customers with annual passes and expediting their entry.

Speedy procession of queues is also a key concern for the commercial aviation industry. FRT is therefore a key component of auto-boarding procedures at a growing number of airports, following pilot projects and trials by airports and airlines around the world. At present, airline travellers can opt in to use facial recognition to register their bag-drop and proceed through entry gates that make quick matches with their electronic passport photos. Technically, the well-lit and controlled environment of airport departure gates offers optimum conditions for FRT – also aided by the high-quality nature of passport photographs. There is much industry enthusiasm for the mainstream roll-out of paperless boarding, with the World Bank funding a 'Known Traveller Digital Identity' project to test the viability of travelling without passports, tickets or boarding passes. Similar systems have been implemented in US cruise ship terminals, as well as train stations and other transit hubs in various Asian cities – all based around passengers being recognized and processed through their faces.

Such applications of facial recognition are often described as part of the broader anticipated capability of the 'smart city' or 'safe city'. Aside from obvious access applications in enclosed public spaces, such as malls, transport hubs and entertainment venues, facial recognition is integrated into various shared open spaces of various 'smart city' infrastructures. Beijing's Haidian district, for example, has installed pilot 'smart' pedestrian crossings, which make use of FRT to deter jaywalking pedestrians. Beijing's Xicheng District added facial recognition capabilities to public rubbish bins that open only if the person is recognized as a local resident. Being recognized by a bin is seen to provide an incentive to be seen to be depositing the correct type of waste into the appropriate receptacle. In all these cases, then, facial recognition offers an unobtrusive way of regulating public behaviours in our increasingly crowded and sped-up urban spaces.

Facial recognition and casinos

Alongside airports and sports stadia, the casino and gaming industry has also proven a key site for the implementation of FRT. Indeed, casinos have long been enthusiastic early adopters of all manner of monitoring and surveillance technology – from CCTV to automated player tracking and floor-management systems. So, too, facial recognition has long been implemented in casino sites, well before the technology was considered reliable enough to be used elsewhere in society. Bally's Las Vegas casino is generally seen to be the first venue to implement a rudimentary facial recognition system back in 1994. By the mid-2000s, around 160 casinos were accessing the Surveillance Information Network, a shared photographic database of more than 2,500 individuals deemed as known 'casino threats' that could be run through facial recognition systems (Norris 2019). Now most large casinos operate some form of facial recognition technology and in some jurisdictions are legally required to do so. All told, keeping tabs on who is entering their premises and monitoring their movements is a familiar element of day-to-day operations within a casino. Consequently, the casino industry has steadily developed a variety of uses for FRT, illustrating the diverse potential of the technology once in situ.

There are many reasons casino operators might want to know who is in their venues and why. For example, most casinos maintain blacklists of previously troublesome individuals whom they consider undesirable to have on the premises. Casinos also operate blacklists of people whom they consider unprofitable to have on the premises. These include known cheaters, as well as 'advantage players' who use legal methods (such as card counting) to stack the odds in their favour. At the same time, there is mounting pressure for the casino industry to enforce 'responsible gaming' procedures. For example, facial recognition is now used to exclude underage and 'impaired' players, and to enforce 'tracked play' conditions where customers are prevented from exceeding pre-agreed time and budget limits. Similarly, FRT is being used to support casinos to participate in the exclusion of self-identified problem gamblers. This allows individuals to join city-wide voluntary exclusion lists and subsequently be denied entry if their resolve weakens. Of course, this function of FRT fits with other more profitable applications of the technology. For example, FRT can be a discreet way of recognizing VIP guests and other high-spending customers at the door, and quickly whisk them away from the general melee. As one marketing pitch puts it, 'Facial recognition ensures that your high rollers or whales are not ignored!' (SAFR 2021).

Recently, casino facial recognition has diversified from using live video streams taken from site-wide camera systems. Konomi – one of the world's largest producers of slot machines and other self-service gaming machines – has started to install discrete facial recognition cameras into its casino machines. Through their SYNK Vision system, these machines can now greet a player by name, display adverts for their favourite food and drink, offer loyalty scheme points, as well as preventing them from playing if they are underage or a registered problem gambler. The Australian firm TabCorp, which is the country's largest gambling company, has trialled FRT to deter underage clients entering betting shops increasingly stocked with self-service gambling machines (Hatch 2019). In all these forms, the continued take-up of facial recognition across the gaming industry is largely welcomed. It is presumed that anyone entering a casino fully expects to be surveilled. It is presumed that honest gamblers are likely to welcome any cheaters being rejected from the premises. It is also claimed that problem gamblers are almost always relieved to be excluded – as one news report put it, 'detected problem gamblers [a]re almost always appreciative of staff's intervention' (*Adelaide Advertiser* 2019).

Facial recognition and retail

As these previous examples illustrate, FRT is a ready means of boosting the operation of public spaces where monitoring and surveillance are already seen as important, and when monitoring and surveillance systems are already in place. As such, another prominent application for FRT has been to augment retail stores' use of CCTV to identify and deter shoplifting – what is known in the trade as retail security. Now, through services such as the United Kingdom's Facewatch system, even small supermarkets can run facial recognition systems that trigger an alert to the shopkeeper as soon as a match is made between someone entering the store and a known subject of interest on Facewatch's national database (as well as any other person that each store has added to its own local 'watchlist').

Yet, as is the case with casinos, once facial recognition technology is in place for one purpose, a range of other uses come to the fore. The result is that customer-facing retail applications are becoming a booming area for the facial recognition industry. For example, small stores are beginning to use FRT to assess customer satisfaction. At the beginning of the 2020s, 7-Eleven stores in Australia introduced a basic iPad-based facial recognition RateIt app to allow customers to provide feedback on the quality of their experience. This system was designed to recognize repeat customers by their facial features and also delineate the opinions and experiences of hard-to-reach but potentially lucrative non-loyalty customers. More ambitiously, Walmart patented facial detection technology to gauge satisfaction levels simply from monitoring the facial expressions of shoppers waiting in checkout queues.

Another major retail development is the use of FRT across different retail sectors to facilitate payment for goods. 'Facial authentication' technology has already been taken up by banks and other services where verifying customer identity is a regular requirement. Following this lead, various retailers are also beginning to implement 'smart store' technology. Clothing retailers such as Jack & Jones and Vero Moda now operate stores in China where shoppers who are members of WeChat's AI Club can fast-track their payments using facial recognition. Similarly, Japanese 7-Eleven stores and US CaliBurger fast-food restaurants are beginning to make use of facial recognition payment through self-service kiosks and tablets. In China, the Alibaba e-commerce company has successfully run trials of its 'Smile to Pay' service for facial recognition payments.

As might be expected, the logic of these facial recognition applications has shifted from helping customers spend money more easily to encouraging customers to spend more money. As such, FRT is being used to provide shoppers with personalized marketing and retail services, what is referred to by marketers as 'Know Your Customer' (KYC). In terms of retail outlets, FRT can be combined with a customer's 'store loyalty' profiling so that shops can recognize frequent customers in the store and provide personalized advertising and other 'customized responses'. In terms of advertising, stores can now display personalized advertising on interactive digital advertising billboards. Indeed, companies such as Cooler Screens now provide in-store advertising that responds to the 'facial profiling' of customers' age, gender and mood. Borrowing from strategies used to maintain online customer interest when browsing retailing websites, physical stores are now using facial recognition systems to send tailored text messages to recognized customers offering on-the-spot discounts and product recommendations based on their prior purchases. These KYC logics have extended to all manner of places where people are encouraged to spend money. For example, the Churchix facial recognition system is now used by more than 2,000 churches in the United States to monitor congregation attendance. This system is also used to highlight regular attendees who might be worth approaching for donations, as well as irregular attendees who might be persuaded to attend church more frequently.

Facial recognition and schools

Enthusiasm for the public application of FRT extends well beyond churches, refugee camps and rubbish bins. Notably, education is another domain where FRT is being steadily adapted for various reasons – ranging from benign instances of letting students use 'face ID' to pay for canteen meals and check out library books through to detecting potential school shooters and other unauthorized campus incursions. Indeed, perhaps the most prominent application of facial recognition technology in US schools is as protection against school campus incursions. Thousands of schools now have facial recognition systems to identify unauthorized intruders and make use of video object classification trained to detect gun-shaped objects, alongside more subtle forms of 'anomaly detection', such as students arriving at school who are dressed differently from normal or carrying oversized bags. The ongoing fear of school shootings has proved to be a marketing point for the US surveillance industry, which has proposed the combination of security cameras and AI as a means of compensating for the failure of legislators to pass meaningful gun-control legislation.

Alongside these security purposes, a variety of FRT applications are now being developed and sold to schools for pedagogical purposes. One emerging application of facial recognition in schools is attendance monitoring, promising to avoid the inevitable gaps and omissions that arise when human teachers are tasked with repeatedly conducting registration of large student groups. For example, the Australian LoopLearn facial recognition roll-call system has been marketed on the grounds of saving up to 2.5 hours of teacher time per week. Elsewhere, automated registration systems are also considered an effective means of overcoming problems of 'fake attendance' and 'proxies', especially in countries such as India where fraudulent school attendance is commonplace (Wagh et al. 2015).

Beyond campus-based security and tracking physical bodies, facial recognition is also being used in a number of virtual-learning contexts. For example, facial recognition systems are now being developed as a means of ensuring the integrity of various aspects of online courses. This includes controlling access to online educational content (Montgomery and Marais 2014), as well as using webcam-based facial recognition to authenticate online learners – in other words, confirming that the students engaging in online learning activities are actually who they claim to be (Valera, Valera and Gelogo 2015). Similarly, there is growing interest in using facial recognition technology to allow students to take formal examinations from their homes. The take-up of 'online proctoring' technology has been hastened by the rise of remote learning in the wake of COVID-19. Now students can replicate exam conditions through their webcam, with FRT being used to remotely identify test takers and then monitor the exam process for any malpractice.

There is also growing interest in facial detection techniques as an indicator of student engagement and learning. Research and development in this area has long suggested that detecting momentary 'facial actions' can provide rich insights into students' (non-)engagement with online learning environments – highlighting episodes of boredom, confusion, delight, flow, frustration and surprise (Dewan, Murshed and Lin 2019). Particularly telling facial actions with regards to learning are reckoned to include brow raising, eyelid tightening and mouth dimpling (e.g. Grafsgaard et al. 2013). Elsewhere, it is claimed that 'facial micro-expression states' (facial states lasting less than half a second) correlate strongly with conceptual learning and 'could perhaps give us a glimpse into what learners [a]re thinking' (Liaw, Chiu and Chou 2014). All told, there is growing educational interest in the face as a 'continuous and non-intrusive way of . . . understand[ing] certain facets of the learner's current state of mind' (Dewan, Murshed and Lin 2019). These experimental findings have led some educationalists to enthusiastically anticipate facial learning detection being deployed on a mass scale. As Timms (2016: 712) reasons, it might soon be possible to gain a real-time sense of which groups of students are in a 'productive state' and of other instances 'where the overall activity is not productive'.

Facial recognition in the workplace

Finally, another key area of adoption is the rising use of FRT in what is termed 'workplace management'. One obvious application of the technology relates to managing workplace access. The past few years has seen growing interest in 'facial access control', especially with regards to sensitive, secure and sterile work environments. For example, the IT firm Intel introduced facial recognition access to prevent 'high-risk individuals' gaining access to its headquarters of over 20,000 employees – including the deterrence of risks such as disgruntled ex-employees and industrial espionage (Rogoway 2020). As might be expected, facial access has enjoyed an accelerated uptake in the aftermath of the COVID-19 pandemic, which has led to increased interest in touchless technologies. Besides its public health advantages, facial recognition access systems are also sold on the grounds of recognizing repeat visitors, and therefore as offering a convenient way of managing access for contractors, temporary staff and regular delivery people.

Another workplace application involves the use of FRT for employee monitoring. One basic application is the use of FRT for identifying which employees have turned up to work. 'Facial time attendance' technology was adopted initially in industries where employees' on-site locations are not permanent, such as building and factory work. These are also places which might traditionally have workplace cultures of people clocking in for absent colleagues. Where workers are paid by the hour, facial time attendance systems can also feed into companies' payroll software. Such systems are sold on the promise of both saving companies money in terms of absenteeism and of ensuring that hard-working staff are not underpaid – especially if they are working overtime. Facial recognition cameras also have a role to play in affect management because of their ability to monitor expression and attentiveness. The Chinese subsidiary of the tech company Canon, for example, has installed cameras equipped with 'smile recognition' into its offices to gauge the perceived mood of the workplace. As one news report put it, 'the cameras only let smiling workers enter rooms or book meetings, ensuring that every employee is definitely, 100 percent happy all the time' (Vincent 2021).

Such work-related uses extend into the application of FRT to support human resource departments and the recruitment of future employees (what is termed 'Know Your Candidate' features). In a basic sense, facial recognition tools are now used to allow recruiters to verify the identity of people attending video interviews. More sophisticated systems are also beginning to use facial detection techniques to gauge interviewee's emotions, stress levels, 'liveliness detection' and other data that can contribute to an overall automatically generated 'employability' score. FRT is also proving invaluable for monitoring workers who do not routinely travel into their place of work. The widespread switch to working from home during the COVID pandemic prompted a shift in work cultures that many office-based industries have since continued. However, for high-end finance workers, any homeworking increases the risk of the security of financially sensitive information being compromised. During the pandemic, some high-end financial firms therefore turned to facial recognition to verify the identity of employees accessing its sensitive financial systems from home, regularly checking in to ensure that only authorized personnel were looking at the screens (Webber 2020).

Elsewhere, in terms of working on the move, FRT is also being taken up across the logistics and delivery sector. For example, FRT has been introduced into the truck-driving and haulage industry under the guise of 'transparent logistics' technology. This involves the use of facial recognition systems to verify the identity of long-distance truck drivers – monitoring how long a driver has been driving each day, ensuring that vehicles have not been stolen, and even automatically uploading the driver's preferred apps and settings into the truck's dashboard and controls. In a less sophisticated manner, gig workers for Amazon's Flex service (where individuals deliver Amazon packages using their own cars) are required to upload selfies to their work app, which are then verified by FRT to confirm their identity. This ensures that multiple people are not sharing the same account, and that only authorized drivers are delivering packages. Amazon has also required its delivery drivers (on penalty of losing their jobs) to consent to the use of facial recognition technology to monitor them while they drive in anticipation of the installation of cameras that 'are able to sense when a driver yawns, appears distracted, or isn't wearing a seatbelt' and can also monitor drivers' body and facial movements (Gurley 2021).

Justifying 'good' uses of facial recognition

These uses of facial recognition are accompanied by many other specialized applications that add to what developers and vendors are keen to promote as everyday innocuous applications of the technology. For example, FRT is being used to authenticate the online identity of everyone from doctors taking medical exams through to people applying for gun licences. It is also used to verify patients receiving hospital treatment to ensure that the correct person is receiving treatment. The technology can be used to facilitate access to government services for those with disabilities that make it difficult to use other forms of online access. In terms of entertainment, commemorative photographs are now being sent directly to music festival goers and water-park visitors, while TV streaming services are using FRT to identify which programmes feature your favourite cartoon characters (Borak 2020). Indeed, beyond identifying Asterix and Astroboy, there is a growing range of uses of FRT for non-human identification. This includes conservation-related facial recognition to identify and track individual koalas in

Australia and brown bears in Alaska. Pet insurers are now accepting facial recognition of pet dogs and cats as an alternative to microchipping the animals (Chiu 2020).

All told, there are hundreds of seemingly useful applications of this technology being quietly integrated into our everyday lives. Industry voices expect FRT to increasingly take over our lives 'one convenience at a time'. The promises of convenience, efficiency and assistance offered by such uses could help lower resistance to the use of the technology and smooth the path to its normalization. In a world where we are increasingly accustomed to opening our smartphones with our face, how much more of a stretch is it to begin to open doors or rubbish bins in the same way? In a world where we can set up a new bank account with a selfie, then why not pay for products in the same manner? Who doesn't want to be recognized as a valued customer at their favourite coffee shop and skip the queue? Who doesn't want to be relieved of the hassle of retrieving their tickets or fumbling with cards and wallets when approaching a busy turnstile? In addition to personal convenience, many of the examples just outlined apply to situations and circumstances where the likely outcomes are beneficial on a collective, humane and society-wide basis. It is hard to argue against any means by which a lost child can be found or the spread of an infectious global virus be curtailed. On a somewhat less dramatic level, it is likely that most dog owners would happily spare their pet the suffering of having a microchip inserted.

Many people also have little concern over some of the more security-focused applications of facial recognition in casinos, schools and workplaces. Indeed, many of the more intrusive applications of FRT outlined in this chapter take place in contexts and settings where people have either opted in to being subjected to facial recognition or already expect to be surveilled. Sitting a conventional examination at school or university already involves a high level of scrutiny and monitoring, not least from the gaze of real-life invigilators roaming the examination hall. Using swipe cards to open doors at work already leaves a digital trail of one's movements around a building. Casinos are already places where customers and staff expect to be filmed continuously. Financial traders being monitored when working from home are already working for highly regulated institutions that would otherwise be heavily monitoring their employees on the trading floor to meet compliance obligations.

All told, this is technology that seems to fit seamlessly with established practices, processes and infrastructures in many public places. For example, workplaces and schools have long traditions of routinely collecting and maintaining name-and-face photographic databases of everyone authorized to be there. Crucially, in many countries, the rise of CCTV has already normalized increasingly comprehensive forms of video monitoring throughout the day and has provided a ready-made infrastructure of surveillance cameras that can be augmented with facial recognition capabilities. Once we get beyond the initial 'creepy' feeling that might arise when a billboard in a mall greets us by name, there is perhaps little in these instances of everyday facial recognition that we have not already integrated into our lifestyles and behaviours. If there is little here that is wholly novel, then the case can be made that there is little to be worried about.

On the face of it, these applications seem far removed from the problematic forms of 'cop tech' that have fuelled recent push-backs and controversies regarding FRT in society. Who, after all, does not want to see children kept safe at school or problem gamblers overcome their addictions? What is the harm in automating a customer satisfaction survey? Certainly, the overt rationales behind these technologies are often well intentioned and largely agreeable. Where is the harm in some customers being given VIP treatment, or a store being advised where it could improve its service? Given all of this, the facial recognition industry insiders remain understandably upbeat about the continued growth of this technology: 'Facial recognition is here to stay, and the possibilities for using it are almost endless. The potential of the technology is undeniable, and it has already proven its worth in several sectors. People are accepting of facial recognition, based on the personal security and convenience it offers' (Watts 2019: 8).

Unpacking the pro-social logics of everyday facial recognition

So what do these examples tell us about the presumed 'goods' and 'harms' of FRT? Many of the facial recognition applications just described convey an overriding promise of convenience – not having to wait to pay in a shop, not having to wait to confirm one's identity before boarding a plane. Some of these conveniences are tied up with public health and safety logics – for example, not having to touch a rubbish bin or a possibly infected door handle. Many of these applications of FRT convey a promise of sorting and filtering – distinguishing between those who can enter as opposed to those who cannot, or distinguishing between those who are regular customers as distinct from those who are 'very important'. Many of these applications of FRT convey promises to fill in the uncertainty and knowledge gaps. The presence of facial recognition allows us to know what actually happened or pre-emptively perhaps even stop it from happening. In the case of the retailing examples just outlined, this formula is inverted: 'If only a smart camera had been there, we could have taken advantage of an otherwise missed sales opportunity.' Many of these applications of FRT also convey a promise of encouraging desirable and pro-social behaviours from people in the knowledge that their actions are personally attributable – a pedestrian who will not jaywalk, a gambling addict who will not attempt to gamble, a lorry driver who will not drive for too long without taking a break.

All told, the implicit logics of all these facial recognition applications reiterate the point that FRT is socially complex. Given this book's intention to develop a critical stance, these relatively non-controversial cases can therefore help us gauge the extent to which facial recognition is a technology that might require careful implementation rather than outright banning. Conversely, for those who do not see FRT as especially problematic, reconsidering the criticisms that might be levelled against even these seemingly innocuous cases might help make clearer the strong concerns that others might have with the very existence of this technology. So what problems might be levelled against the forms of facial recognition covered in this chapter?

Facial recognition is fallible

First is the fact that many implementations of FRT simply do not work in the ways promised. In terms of simple bald numbers, while reported levels of false positives and false negatives remain encouraging in statistical terms, they still involve large numbers of people being erroneously 'recognized' by these systems in real life. Even the use of FRT to aid airport boarding reports success rates 'well in excess' of 99 per cent – i.e. wrongly preventing one in every hundred passengers boarding the plane. If FRT does not work perfectly in an airport, then it will not work perfectly in any other setting. As was noted earlier, airports boast the ideal conditions for FRT in terms of well-lit settings, high-quality passport photographs, high-spec cameras and static, compliant passengers wanting to be recognized by the camera and authenticate their identity. Error rates are considerably higher for FRT systems that are not located within such ideal conditions.

Whether or not you are concerned by not being allowed on a plane at the first attempt probably depends on how often this inconvenience occurs. Other system failures can have more alarming consequences: people being denied access to benefits or, as in the case of Uber drivers, access to their work. When a face recognition system fails, it can be

onerous and time consuming to prove that the machine is
wrong. Moreover, most of the trial programs and test cases
described in this chapter continue to show the propensity of
FRT to misrecognize certain groups of people over others.
For example, trials of FRT continue to show a propensity
to misrecognize people of colour, especially women (see
Buolamwini and Gebru 2018). Similarly, these systems
continue to work less successfully with people wearing head
coverings and veils, and those with facial tattoos – in other
words, people who do not conform to 'majority' appearance
in many parts of the world. As Shoshana Magnet (2011:
5) notes in her work on biometric failure, 'Biometric repre-
sentations of the body also produce new forms of identity,
including unbiometrifiable bodies that cannot be recognized
by these new identification technologies, a subject identity
that has profound implications for individuals' ability to
work, to collect benefits, and to travel across borders.'

Some failures may seem less consequential, but they pose
their own challenges. Not being immediately recognized
as a theme-park season-ticket holder or a frequent flyer is
unlikely to lead to serious inconvenience or long-term harm.
Yet these misrecognitions and denials might well constitute a
further micro-aggression in a day already replete with them.
In celebrating the conveniences of contactless payments and
skipping queues, we need to remember that FRTs are not
experienced by every user as making everyday life smoother,
frictionless and more convenient.

More generally, there is little evidence that many of these
systems are actually leading to pronounced efficiencies or
improved outcomes. To date, there has been no confirmed
prevention of a school shooting using FRT. Indeed, the
capacity of facial recognition systems to actually prevent
hostile shooters has been criticized as little more than
security theatre, with the technology argued to 'offer only
the appearance of safer schools' (Andrew Ferguson cited in
Harwell 2018). Similarly, while Moscow authorities claimed
to have been able to manage COVID quarantine through

FRT, doubts were quickly raised over the effectiveness and coverage of this system. Instead, it could be argued that the main value of FRT is as a high-profile way that authorities can be seen to be 'doing something' about a social problem or challenge. Put bluntly, there is no quick computer-based solution to preventing determined school intruders or the spread of a virus. Most experts agree that the most expedient method to reduce US school shootings would be to reform gun-control laws. The best way of encouraging people to conform to quarantine measures is by having a strong community ethos. The danger of relying on comprehensive surveillance is that it could have an indirect effect on such an ethos – promising to render it less necessary and even fostering forms of mutual mistrust.

Thus, while we might accept that surveillance has a role to play in securing society, this does not always mean that more of it is better. As Kelly Gates (2011: 197–8) observes, 'The most stable, peaceful societies are not societies in which everyone is identifiable all the time everywhere they go. Instead, they are societies in which social and cultural differences are respected, and people have a healthy measure of autonomy and control over their own lives.' Only perfect surveillance can make up for the total absence of trust, and there is no such thing as perfect surveillance. The ways in which FRTs come together with contemporary forms of 'techno-solutionism' should not be overlooked.

Facial recognition is intrusive

It is important to raise questions concerning just how unobtrusive all these facial recognition applications actually are in practice. Indeed, one of the big promises of FRT is its seamless automation of the processes of recognizing a face and triggering an appropriate response. However, many of the systems described in this chapter are far from fully automated. In many cases, presenting one's face to a camera simply triggers a prompt for a human worker to do something.

Astra Taylor (2018) refers to this as 'fauxtomation' – the illusion of having automated systems that run automatically but actually require large amounts of concealed human labour to carry out their function. In one sense, then, we need to remain mindful of how facial recognition technologies do not simply 'function' of their own accord in settings such as sports stadia, schools or airports. Instead, the introduction of a new system or technology requires an extensive human infrastructure to mediate, moderate and troubleshoot its demands and quirks (see Mateescu and Elish 2019). Yet this example raises a number of concerns – noting that this work is often underpaid (or not paid at all), carried out by women, not valued by those investing in these expensive technologies, 'reinforcing the illusion that machines are smarter than they really are' (Taylor 2018).

Aside from these concerns over the additional labour required to keep FRT running is the dehumanizing and exhausting work that those people whose faces are being subjected to FRT are also required to engage in. Consider, for example, how these systems constitute very reductive processes of 'recognition' in contrast to how they would ordinarily be viewed by a human. People are not 'seen' by facial recognition technologies in a manner that is able to discern their full range of facial emotions. One practical consequence of facial recognition technologies is people having to contort their facial expressions in unnatural ways that allow the technology to 'detect' and/or 'recognize' them. If the cold algorithmic gaze of the system is not triggered, then the onus is on the individual in front of the camera to present a different (more 'readable') face. While these adjustments might seem like minor inconveniences, it could be argued that the lack of full acknowledgement of what are amongst any individual's most personal attributes is inevitably dehumanizing and distancing. Of course, being required to present your 'best face' or 'put on a brave face' is not a new thing. We are continually performing with our faces in social situations – not appearing too bored in a job interview or looking amused when being told an anecdote. Nevertheless, having to regularly perform these faux-emotions to a machine is an extra layer of labour, often with a less socially affirming response.

Another obtrusive element of FRT is the curtailment of one's right to obscurity while in different social settings. The more widespread deployment of FRT means that workers, shoppers, pedestrians and sports fans are now finding it increasingly difficult to blend into the background, take a back seat and generally go about their business under the radar. This development threatens the ability of people to manage what is known and disclosed about them, and to find ways to ensure that their actions and intentions are correctly interpreted and understood. This raises the contention that people have a right to 'mental privacy' or, in human rights terminology, the *forum internum*. This refers to an individual's right to not have their actions, intentions, moods and emotions constantly subjected to public scrutiny without their control. For example, not everyone will want to have their previous purchasing history made visible as they pass a billboard. Not everyone will be comfortable with the idea that waiting in line for the checkout involves having their face monitored for signs of any emotion.

Facial recognition and function creep

Many of the examples in the chapter also point to the tendency of FRT to be adopted for an expanding range of purposes – what might be termed 'function creep'. For example, scanning the faces of casino guests to self-exclude problem gamblers fits with other uses that casino owners might welcome. As noted earlier, facial recognition can be a discreet way of recognizing VIP guests and other lucrative 'high rollers' at the door who can quickly be whisked away from the general melee. This logic could easily be extended into recognizing (and deterring) repeat customers who spend only small amounts of money, or croupiers whose tables are not particularly profitable. What if every vending machine could recognize customers before displaying prices? A machine that could adjust the prices based on information about customers' incomes might be programmed to serve as Robin Hood and charge the wealthy more to subsidize the less fortunate. The more likely outcome, however, would be to attempt to extract from every consumer as much as they would be willing to pay over the standardized price at any given moment. It is easy to envision systems that gauge the motivation of a purchaser at a particular moment, subject to environmental conditions ('how thirsty and hot do they appear on a sweltering day?' and so on).

This tendency for function creep extends to the implementation of facial recognition in many different sectors. For example, a few months after developing their facial recognition and geolocation-based Home Quarantine Tracking System during the COVID pandemic, police forces in Pune and Maharashtra repurposed the application into something called ExTra (Externees Monitoring and Tracking System). This ensured that criminals who had been externed from local jurisdictions were not infringing their exclusion orders. The system included scheduled and 'surprise' requests for externees to upload selfies to confirm their location (*Indian Express* 2020).

This latter example illustrates how the logics of monitoring, recording, tracking and profiling are likely to exacerbate (and certainly not mitigate) the authoritarian tendencies of the places within which they are implemented. This is perhaps easy to imagine if we are talking about the use of FRT by a police force or within a prison. However, in terms of this chapter's examples, it is also important to consider the authoritarian tendencies of schools, casinos and supermarkets. For example, while a 7-Eleven store might not appear particularly authoritarian to a customer entering a consumer satisfaction rating, it remains a hierarchized and ordered workplace for those behind the tills. While 7-Eleven's RateIt system was designed to capture the opinions and experiences of hard-to-reach but potentially lucrative non-loyalty customers, the system was also designed to monitor workers – with customers invited to rate the performance of individual staff members. Moreover, the specific addition of FRT was also intended to control the actions of staff working at the store. Staff members' photographs were also included in this system, and the facial recognition element of the system functioned to prevent staff from 'gaming' the system by entering bogus customer ratings of their own performance, as well as preventing their friends or associates from entering more than one rating in a 24-hour period (Taylor 2021).

The underpinning logics of control

These latter examples highlight the tensions between convenience and control that underpin any surveillance technology such as facial recognition. For example, one of the claims for many of the cases of facial recognition described in this chapter is that they are entered into by choice – or at the very least do not involve identifying large groups of unwitting people. Many of the examples in this chapter are what vendors refer to as 'closed loop' systems. At present, you have to opt to make a payment by face and register your details in advance. A school's facial recognition attendance-monitoring system will only be looking for the faces of the 30 students who are registered in the class. A search for a missing child is only looking to match faces with one identifiable photograph – this system will only 'recognize' you if you are the missing child.

Yet the nature of these 'choices' is dependent on the context. School students do not have a choice to attend school or not, let alone whether to take an online examination or not if that is what has been stipulated. Most supermarket customers do not have a choice whether to buy groceries or not, any more than refugees have a meaningful choice when seeking aid and shelter in a refugee camp. As such, we need to remain mindful of the ways in which any application of FRT is entwined with the power relations of the settings it is being used in. Take, for instance, the underpinning logic of using FRT to 'sort' people. Of course, most people would not raise objections to sorting who is able to access their bank account as opposed to who is not. Yet the examples of facial recognition outlined throughout this chapter highlight a range of reasons for wanting to sort people into categories – the unauthorized, the untrustworthy, the potentially dangerous, the vulnerable or simply people whom a commercial organization might profit from recognizing.

The role played by facial recognition in enabling social sorting highlights the unequal power relations inherent in the logic of its deployment. The power dynamic between those being sorted and those doing the sorting is clearly unbalanced. FRTs are mostly focused on people who are in the compliant and/or disempowered position of wanting to gain entry (to their bank account or a casino), being held against their will, or not being able to control their actions. Consider, for example, the humanitarian use of FRT with refugee populations. Such applications of facial recognition have been described as part of an insidious 'techno-colonialism', reinvigorating historical colonial relationships of dependency with the added complication of IT industry involvement and the logics of humanitarian aid. All told, facial recognition does little to disrupt power asymmetries between refugees and aid agencies and ultimately might be seen to become constitutive of humanitarian crises themselves (Madianou 2019). Such concerns have led to high-profile calls for a moratorium on the use of facial recognition with refugees. As UN's special rapporteur Tendayi Achiume reasons, 'Data collection is not an apolitical exercise . . . especially when powerful global north actors collect information on vulnerable populations with no regulated methods of oversight and accountability' (Achiume 2020).

Examples such as this remind us that there is no such thing as a neutral or natural set of sorting criteria. Instead, technologies designed to recognize and sort people will always represent a defined set of interests. All too often, however, the automated system renders these interests non-transparent or frames them (falsely) as the result of an objective, machinic process untainted by particular interests. Moreover, facial recognition can easily shift the burden of proof onto those in the most vulnerable positions, least equipped to take it on. In Australia, for example, a program to assess whether people had received government benefits in excess of their eligible amounts wrongly billed hundreds of thousands of people for having received overpayments. The burden fell upon those who are already under-resourced to prove that the system was wrong.

Challenging the idea of facial recognition 'for good'

These criticisms certainly muddy any preconceptions that we might have about whether FRT is an inherently 'good' or wholly 'bad' thing. Certainly, the idea of using FRT as an alternative to microchipping a pet dog or of making sure that supermarket workers are not underpaid seem relatively uncontroversial (and even welcome) developments. However, the underlying message from some critics remains that any 'added value' or gained 'efficiencies' are outweighed by the broader consequences of having these technologies in our everyday lives. What might appear to be the relatively benign implementation of facial technology in everyday social settings could amount to a case of what Luke Stark (2019: 54) terms 'trading off its enormous risks for relatively meagre gains'. This prospective trade-off raises the concern that casinos, schools and supermarkets are being co-opted as sites for the normalization of what is a 'societally dangerous' technology – examples of what Stark (2019: 55) describes as 'facial privacy loss leaders'. For this reason, we need to think very carefully about how readily we might want to embrace these technologies, even in contexts which seem relatively benign and 'low stakes'. If these uses open the way for the more general and widespread use of FRT, then it can be strongly argued that schools, pedestrian crossings and casinos should not be places where communities become desensitized to being automatically identified, tracked and profiled by a technology that remains capable of being used for much more harmful purposes.

This formulation brings us back full circle to the wider question: 'Do we need facial recognition at all in contemporary society?' Certainly, many of the pitches for FRT products as described in this chapter are contestable. Boarding a plane, paying for groceries and registering a class of students are all events that can already take place relatively easily and quickly without FRT. We already have developed convenient ways of unlocking our smartphones, giving customer feedback and keeping tabs on who gains entry to casinos. Many of the proposed use cases for facial recognition technology come across as high-tech solutions in search of a problem. Indeed, the development of the technology participates in a familiar cycle of acceleration and streamlining. Once facial recognition systems are deployed to speed transit, the rhythm and volume of transit accelerates correspondingly, extenuating the need for the tool that enabled this shift. Once it is removed, the system would break down.

These examples also raise key questions of trust. How much trust do we have in the institutions that are taking the lead in deploying the technology? Can we trust them to continue to use it in good faith, rather than getting tempted by its power to de-anonymize the world? How far do we trust institutions not to indulge in 'function creep'? For example, supermarkets might well want to identify disgruntled customers, perhaps to push particular advertising messages to them or perhaps to dissuade them from returning. To what extent can we trust these institutions to recognize the shortcomings of these systems? Even if we can trust the shops, schools or churches that are using FRT, to what extent can we trust the technology companies behind the scenes to also be acting in good faith – i.e. in terms of reusing and repurposing all the personal data they are collecting? Based on recent events, the most obvious answer might well be not at all.

Conclusions

In many ways, the key battlegrounds where the societal role of FRT will be determined are precisely the types of mundane applications reviewed in this chapter. Regardless of its use by law enforcement and military authorities, this technology is already finding a place in retail, banking, transport and workplaces. FRT is already becoming woven into the fabric of our everyday lives, and a whole generation is becoming familiar and comfortable with it. Thus a critical discussion of FRT needs to start from the point of considering what possible uses of FRT *might* be acceptable. Why might we not accept the missing child scenario or the microchipping of our pets? If these are acceptable, then why not extend this to rubbish-bin monitoring or personalized shopping? Is it possible to imagine future applications of the technology that might be considered permissible? For example, Luke Stark concedes one potential use of FRT that might be considered permissible under tight regulations is as an accessibility tool for the visually impaired – for example, to identify non-speaking work colleagues or classmates for them during group meetings. In the same manner, then, might there be valid uses for those with prosopagnosia – those not able to recognize their own faces or others?

Of course, there are growing numbers of critics who now contend that there is no room at all for any incarnation of FRT – however benign it might appear, and whatever conveniences it might promise. The main logic here is that any 'non-controversial' iterations of FRT are simply paving the way for much more pernicious and oppressive forms. As Sarah Hamid reasons, FRT is so fundamentally oppressive that it needs to be approached from an abolitionist perspective – recognizing that any roll-out of this technology remains fundamentally a carceral technology:

> These technologies never exist without their carceral counterpart ... We recognize facial recognition technology, a weapon used by law enforcement to identify, profile, and enact violence against categories of people. So individuals opting in to unlock their phones with facial recognition serves to improve a technology that has necessarily violent implications – individuals opting in, in other words, are participating in the creation and refinement of this weapon. (Hamid 2020)

This argument certainly puts the conveniences, efficiencies and simplicities of the FRTs outlined in this chapter in a very different light. So what other applications of facial recognition are critics such as Hamid, Stark and others referring to? To what extent do these other uses negate any of the promises and conveniences outlined in this chapter? In contrast to this chapter's focus on thinking about 'facial recognition for good', what about the flipside? In short, what problems can arise if our societies fully embrace facial recognition over the next few years?

5

Problematic Applications: Facial Recognition as an Inherent Harm?

Introduction

Identifying pets and paying for a cup of coffee are not the only use cases that come to mind when talking about facial recognition. On the contrary, FRT is often imagined by public, media and policy makers as a technology that raises concerns, suspicions and a general sense of foreboding. Such sentiments were certainly evident in recent protests around North America and Europe against police use of FRT and have pushed governments and industry into the regulations and bans outlined in chapter 3. This chapter considers some of these more concerning ways that facial recognition is beginning to be integrated into our societies. Focusing on these potentially problematic uses therefore provides a counterpoint to the pro-social uses detailed in chapter 4, as well as general enthusiasms within IT industry and computer science communities. As acknowledged from the start of this book, FRT is a highly contested and controversial technology. This chapter takes a deeper look at some of the reasons why this is the case. Why is it that so many people still presume FRT to be a chilling, authoritarian and generally unwelcome oppressive incursion into our everyday lives? How is this technology being developed and used in ways that many people see as inexorably linked to diminished civil rights and increased discrimination?

In contrast to the mundane and pro-social uses of FRT outlined in chapter 4, this chapter tackles what could be described as more alarming uses and applications. In particular, this chapter looks at automated facial recognition through the lens of security and control, as a means of surveillance and even as a source of oppression and harassment. It explores the already diverse application of facial systems by police and security forces, as well as facial recognition applications developed for the military and prison service. It also considers the potential abuses and misuses of FRT by employers and ordinary members of the public. What can we make of claims being made about the harms of facial technology implicit in contexts ranging from securing US borders to driving an Uber? Where are the recurring harms that facial recognition technology is likely to raise – especially for vulnerable populations – and what priorities emerge from this framing? Even if we discount the more speculative fears that often cloud discussions of FRT in terms of future harms, what problems might the technology *already* be associated with?

Police uses of facial recognition

Police and law enforcement agencies feature prominently in the history of facial recognition as some of the earliest adopters and supporters of the technology. Of course, policing has long involved use of biometric information. Police in the United Kingdom and the United States have been using fingerprinting since the turn of the twentieth century, with electronic fingerprint technology developed by Japanese police in the 1980s. Facial recognition is one of a number of biometric technologies now in regular use by police agencies around the world alongside algorithmic fingerprint analysis, palmprints, iris scanning and DNA testing. Recently, police agencies have emerged as early adopters of voice and gait analysis systems. Given that surveillance and identification are key aspects of the work of police agencies, this appetite for new biometrics technology is unsurprising.

Perhaps the most scrutinized police uses of facial recognition have played out in the United States. Until recently, FRT was a relatively routine, if not fully acknowledged, part of US police procedure. As NYPD police commissioner James P. O'Neill argued in a 2019 *New York Times* opinion piece, from a police perspective facial recognition 'has proved its worth as a crime-fighting resource' and was 'a uniquely powerful tool in our most challenging investigations'. Commissioner O'Neill's force has been using FRT since 2011 – mostly for matching faces from CCTV video stills against their extensive database of arrest photographs. Investigators are able to compare any possible matches against what they termed 'open source' images to identify leads (including images they could find on social media). In his piece, O'Neill reckoned that NYPD detectives had gone through this process over 7,000 times over the past 12 months, making 998 arrests from 1,851 possible matches. He also praised the technology for its use in identifying murder victims, as well as clearing suspects who had been wrongly identified by witnesses. All told, as far as most police are concerned, the continued use of facial recognition seems an obvious benefit: 'To keep New York City safe requires enormous and relentless effort. It would be an injustice to the people we serve if we policed our 21st-century city without using 21st-century technology' (O'Neill 2019).

Injustice or not, the accuracy of FRT as a policing tool is under constant challenge. For example, one of the most controversial police uses of FRT is the identification of otherwise unknown suspects. In official terms, the scope of this 'one-to-many' use of facial recognition in many countries is restricted to specific official photo databases. For example, US police and agencies such as the FBI have the capacity to run matches through the Next Generation Identification – Interstate Photo System (NGI-IPS) which contains more than 30 million criminal mugshots. The worldwide equivalent is the INTERPOL Face Recognition System (IFRS), which contains facial images received from more than 179 countries. This database is shared with national police agencies around the world and is claimed to have led to the identification of over 1,000 suspected criminals, fugitives, persons of interest and missing persons.

Yet official databases such as NGI-IPS and IFRS are not the only sources of knowing who a face might belong to. Concerns are raised in some countries where police matches extend beyond images from official law enforcement databases and into nationwide photo databases such as drivers' licences, passports and national ID cards. For example, police forces in some US states are reported to also make use of photos from the Department of Motor Vehicles databases. Some local police forces also maintain their own databases, with the Pinellas County Sheriff's Office in Florida reported to run around 8,000 searches a month on its database of 7 million Florida residents on behalf of around 240 different agencies. This particular county has been amassing this database for more than 20 years since receiving federal funding to start the project.

Further concerns are also raised over other non-official systems and photo databases that some police agencies might also be using. For example, when the customer lists of the controversial Clearview AI application (illicitly using social media photos scraped from the Web, often in violation of platforms' terms of service) were leaked, users included hundreds of US law enforcement agencies. Despite initial denials, these customer lists also exposed users from various federal and state police forces in Australia, New Zealand, the United Kingdom and Europe. The Clearview revelations added to a suspicion that police forces may not be particularly careful about adhering to best practice for the use of such technologies. For example, US police forces using Amazon's Rekognition product were reported to be lowering the default confidence threshold for matches to below the recommended 99 per cent threshold for law enforcement uses (Menegus 2019). This technical argument generates more potential matches, but it also increases the likelihood of false positives where innocent people are identified as possible suspects. More bizarre reports include US police forces running celebrity photographs through their facial recognition systems to find leads. If, for example, a witness says a suspect looked like a celebrity, then the celebrity image can be used to generate matches from a stored database. One well-publicized instance involved the successful tracking down of a Woody Harrelson lookalike by the NYPD. Other police departments admit to running facial recognition matches on composite sketches, or else having to rotate, blur and clone-stamp (by moving information from one part of a photograph to another) images on Photoshop to make them machine readable.

Underlying these speculative (and some would say spurious) practices is a concern that police forces are over-relying on these complex technologies and using them inappropriately to address small-scale incidents, occasionally with incorrect outcomes. Despite guidelines for FRT to be used only in exceptional circumstances, there are numerous reports of US police using the technology to investigate minor offences and pretty crimes. These include reported incidents of Oregon police using Rekognition to clear up a US$12 shoplifting offence in 2018, Tallahassee police using FRT to investigate a 2019 theft of an US$80 smartphone, and Florida police using facial recognition software in a US$50 drug dealing case in 2016. As Valentino-DeVries (2020) notes, the small-scale nature of these instances 'offers insights into which crimes facial recognition is best suited to help solve: shoplifting, check forgery, ID fraud'.

Use of facial recognition by security forces

Aside from the police, FRT is used by various other agencies working in the areas of security and control. In the United States, for example, interested agencies range from the FBI through to Homeland Security and various border agencies. For example, the FBI made headlines in its use of 'open source facial recognition' to identify a rioter from the storming of the US Capitol building in 2021. In this instance, crowdsourced video of the man assaulting police officers was matched with photo images taken from his girlfriend's Instagram posts. In light of the Capitol riots, the US Secret Service (a long-time user of FRT) began to trial a facial recognition system in the White House and its grounds with the declared aim of working out effective ways to assist in 'identifying known subjects of interest prior to initial contact with law enforcement at the White House Complex'.

Another agency with long-standing ties to FRT since the 9/11 attacks is the US Homeland Security agency in its use of FRT to verify entry into the country and to track passengers on planes and other forms of transit. In 2016, the Obama administration signed off plans to deploy biometric identity verification for all international travellers seeking to gain entry into the United States – a scheme that the Trump administration subsequently attempted to expedite to apply to all travellers crossing US borders. While this ambition of complete scanning has since been scaled back, the Department for Homeland Security continues to expand its use of facial recognition to screen travellers. During 2020, the Customs and Border Protection agency was reported to have run facial scans on more than 43.7 million people at border crossings, resulting in the identification of 252 people attempting to enter the United States on stolen or false passports. Under this system, assurances were made that new images of US citizens would only be retained for 12 hours, while information collected from foreign nationals would be kept for 75 years.

Similar forms of facial recognition are deployed by security forces around the world, along with other uses of FRT that prove more controversial to western observers and media. One concerning development is the use of FRT to monitor protests. This was a widely criticized feature of how the Hong Kong authorities handled the pro-democracy protests in 2019 and 2020, during which protesters developed a variety of strategies for thwarting automated facial recognition, including face coverings and laser pointers to dazzle the cameras. Similarly, Moscow authorities' use of the city's network of facial recognition-enabled cameras to identify protesters also drew criticism from commentators upset at the appropriation of a system that had been introduced under the guise of the 2018 FIFA World Cup and then expanded to help track COVID quarantine regulations. Of course, similar occurrences are not unknown in western countries. For example, the arrest of a protester at the 2020 Lafayette Square protests in Washington DC brought to light the existence of the previously little-known National Capital Region Facial Recognition Investigative Leads System (NCR FRILS) – used in this instance to identify an otherwise unknown protester who had assaulted police officers. This aspect of the Lafayette Square protests remained largely overlooked amidst the deployment of the National Guard to protect a bible-waving president standing on the steps of a church to denounce Black Lives Matter protesters. Nevertheless, facial recognition remains a key tool for security forces of all countries, however democratic and open they present themselves to be.

In less dramatic ways, FRT is also becoming established in many 'low-rights' contexts where camera-based surveillance is already the norm. Unsurprisingly, perhaps, one key site of use is prisons and other places of detention. For example, UK prisons have run successful six-week trials to scan faces of prison visitors in an attempt to thwart smuggling of drugs and other contraband to inmates, as well as to identify visitors to the prison using false identification documents. Commercial FRT systems are now being sold to prison authorities on the promise of alerting guards when 'known criminals' come to visit inmates, to verify the location of prisoners at all times, and even to double-check the identification of prisoners prior to their release. Such uses are exemplified in China's flagship 'smart prison' in Yancheng. This prison is designed to continuously monitor its 'high-status inmates' through networked cameras and sensors. FRT is used to flag suspicious behaviour (including unethical interactions with prison guards such as bribe taking) and to gain credence for the prison's boast that it is using technology to 'make prison breaks impossible' (Chen 2019).

Perhaps the most widely criticized application of FRT by security services is its use by Chinese authorities in their monitoring and suppression of the Muslim Uyghur ethnic group in north-western China. China has long been accused of sustained human rights abuses against the Uyghur population, including extensive surveillance and deportation to forced labour camps and re-education programmes. These tactics have made increasing use of facial recognition for minority identification purposes. For example, security agencies in a number of large cities across Western China have been reported to use facial recognition to identify Uyghurs, with authorities in Sanmenxia reportedly running as many as 500,000 facial scans in one month in efforts to audit whether or not residents were Uyghurs (Mozur 2019a). In response, Chinese facial recognition firms looking to market their products to state authorities have begun to include the stated capacity to detect Uyghur ethnicity as part of their product development. Internal documents from the large Chinese IT firm Huawei reportedly made mention of a 'Uyghur alert' product, while Huawei product patents have outlined profiling capabilities to discern 'race' categories, including the ability to distinguish between Han and Uyghur ethnic identity.

Military uses of facial recognition

As highlighted in previous chapters, facial recognition is a technology born out of military support – not least from substantial funding from the US Defense Advanced Research Project Agency and the Army Research Laboratory to initiate the development of FRT in the absence of any obvious commercial market. These investments have subsequently led to the US military (as well as military forces elsewhere in the world) emerging as a significant consumer and user of FRT. For example, military bases and garrisons are beginning to use FRT for gatekeeping and sentry duties – what is sold to military customers as 'tireless sentry' technology. In mid-2021, the US Army issued a call to install facial recognition at the entry points of all its bases. The military are also beginning to take up various forms of mobile FRT designed to be deployed in encampment, patrol and battlefield contexts. These range from apps to allow soldiers to identify people they come across as either friend or foe through to FR-enabled long-range biometric binoculars and night-vision systems (using infrared imaging) to allow soldiers to identify 'people of interest'.

As with the use of facial recognition on civilian populations, these military surveillance activities are underpinned by large photographic databases. For example, the US Army's Video Identification, Collection, and Exploitation (VICE) software is used to identify individuals who are deemed to be potential threats to Department of Defense missions. VICE comprises over 25,000 biometric records which are matched to the Pentagon's Biometrically Enabled Watchlists of people considered to pose a potential risk to US defence operations. In addition to VICE, the US Army also makes use of an Automated Biometric Information System comprising 7.4 million biometric profiles of people who have interacted with US military overseas. This includes profiles of allied soldiers and civilian personnel, as well as combatants and members of opposing forces and terrorist groups. This database includes face profiles, alongside fingerprint and DNA data, what has been described as 'a biometric dragnet of anyone who has come in contact with the US military abroad' (Gershgorn 2019).

The military are understandably keen to promote the benefits of these facial recognition efforts. As the director of the US Defense Forensics and Biometrics Agency put it in sabre-rattling terms, 'Denying our adversaries anonymity allows us to focus our lethality. It's like ripping the camouflage netting off the enemy ammunition dump.' In this sense, biometrics plays a key part in the tactical aim of American forces to establish identity dominance, as evident in US military claims during the 2001–2021 occupation of Afghanistan to have had comprehensive knowledge of up to 80 per cent of the population in order to know who local people were and what was their previous involvement in insurgency (Guo and Noor 2021). Yet, as with use of FRT by the FBI and police, concerns are raised over the non-accountability and lack of transparency of these military programs. As Gershgorn (2019) puts it, these databases and watchlists constitute 'a large and quickly growing network of surveillance systems operated by the US military and present anywhere the United States has deployed troops, vacuuming up biometric data on millions of unsuspecting individuals'.

Alongside these current surveillance and security applications, it is also worth paying attention to the US military's investment in facial recognition research and development. This includes the US Army Research Laboratory's development of the Visible-Thermal Face Dataset. This comprises more than half a million images of 395 different faces designed to help train FRT for identifying people in the dark. Similarly, since 2016 the Advanced Tactical Facial Recognition at a Distance Technology project has been working on the development of portable devices capable of identifying individuals from a distance of one kilometre. Another long-running area of work is the integration of FRT within the US Army's fleet of more than 8,000 drones and unmanned aerial vehicles. Of course, these ambitions are not unique to the US Army and are being pursued by military forces all around the world. In addition, private contractors and commercial start-ups are also involved in developing these products. For example, the Israeli defence contractor Rafael Advanced Defense Systems has partnered with the AnyVision computer vision company to set up SightX. This aims to incorporate facial and object recognition into drones and ground-robot technologies, promising the capacity to efficiently and accurately 'differentiate between innocent civilians and militants' (Pivcevic 2021).

In one sense, labelling these uses of FRT as 'harms' seems less applicable to the military as compared to civilian agencies – after all, one of the key functions of military forces is to do harm. Yet such uses of FRT are complicated further in countries where the military are entwined with authoritarian regimes. During the civil unrest against the 2021 Myanmar coup, the severe handling of protests saw military forces using FRT alongside stun grenades, tear gas, rubber bullets and drone surveillance. Some of the thousands of arrests of anti-coup protesters in Naypyidaw were initiated by the military regime's use of the city's network of facial recognition-enabled CCTV cameras installed earlier as part of the Safe City program. The fact that authoritarian regimes and military dictatorships are taking the lead in the widespread use of the technology to stifle dissent and control the population should give the rest of the world pause when it comes to contemplating the widespread use of automated facial recognition.

Use of facial recognition at work and home

Many of the cases raised so far in this chapter relate to clear instances of security and control in areas of society that are predicated upon surveillance, monitoring and identification of individuals. Notwithstanding the appropriateness of their actual uses of facial recognition, one would not expect the military, police or security forces to be deploying technology in completely benign ways. However, there is a long-standing pattern of military surveillance technologies migrating into civilian use over time. At the same time, it is worth considering the use of facial recognition in more conventional everyday contexts that nonetheless convey a similar sense of surveillance and control. In short, it is worth considering why the reasons that might prompt us to feel uneasy about FRT being (mis)used in prisons, law enforcement and battlefield contexts may spill over into more mundane applications of FRT in our immediate surroundings.

As described in chapter 4, a number of facial recognition applications are beginning to be deployed in the workplace as a means of employee monitoring. We have already outlined the use of FRT for employee attendance tracking, time recording (clocking in) and monitoring compliance with various safety and security protocols. Yet these uses also extend into adopting facial recognition to more closely monitor employee activity and productivity. For example, combined with keystroke monitoring, facial recognition technology makes it possible to extensively monitor the time spent 'on task' of office workers when working from home. This might discourage workers from taking time away from their computers. This logic of 'employee recognition' technology extends beyond the monitoring of white-collar workers to the monitoring of low-paid insecure work. For example, FRT is now used to monitor the activity and productivity of warehouse workers, delivery drivers and many other forms of gig work. Indeed, as discussed briefly in chapter 4, in many countries Uber drivers are required to sign in for a shift by uploading a face shot on their smartphone – starting work once the app has verified their identity (what Uber refers to as a 'real-time ID check').

Another growth area of FRT systems is the home market, with various manufacturers producing low-cost home security systems with facial recognition capabilities. Homeowners are now using Wi-Fi-enabled high-definition camera systems that can send alerts when a person arrives on their doorstep and determine whether the individual is known to the homeowner or not. Google's Nest Cam boasts the capacity to identify unknown visitors from up to 50 feet away, with the Nest Aware sending Familiar Face Alerts to users' phones as soon as known people are recognized. Other systems provide indoor facial recognition. For anyone with an inclination towards low-cost total surveillance, these systems can run up to a dozen separate facial recognition cameras around a house and its surrounding outside spaces.

This level of security raises concerns over misuse of these systems by homeowners for vigilantism and other forms of harassment against anyone deemed to be undesirable in their neighbourhood. Concerns are also raised in terms of images being shared with law enforcement agencies – with outward-facing front-door cameras constituting unregulated local networks of facial recognition surveillance that might be accessible to the police. More intimately, home FRT also fits into wider trends in digital domestic abuse and 'technology facilitated coercive control', not least the capacity to more closely track movements and actions of family members (Dragiewicz et al. 2018). As with other digital monitoring systems, the domestication of these surveillance technologies works both to normalize their use by authorities and to align the attitudes and imperatives of users with those of police and intelligence agencies. In a climate of increased perceived risk, this technology offers the prospect (if not necessarily the reality) of greater control by incorporating the tools used by 'the professionals' into one's domestic life. In so doing, one takes on the role of securing one's home and family in ways that align with the exercise of state power and control.

Following this logic, one of the main concerns arising from facial recognition applications such as PimEyes and Clearview AI based on the illicit scraping of photos from social media is the potential use of these services by individuals for stalking and harassment. In 2020, digital rights activists exposed an illegal trade in running face-matching searches from Moscow's extensive CCTV network of surveillance cameras (Brandom 2020). For a fee of around 16,000 roubles (US$200), a photo match could be run and details supplied of a selected person's movements around the city over the past month. While it is not clear whether this was achieved through hacking or bribery of security officials, the capacity for any individual to track a stranger based on a snapshot of their face is open to obvious forms of abuse. As Maya Shwayder (2020) reasons, 'this kind of facial-recognition technology could be a boon to stalkers, people with a history of domestic abuse, and anyone else who would want to find out everything about you for a nefarious purpose.'

Reassessing the various 'harms' associated with these applications of facial recognition

In many ways, the concerns raised by the cases of facial recognition use just outlined echo long-standing concerns over other forms of surveillance relating to the changing nature of power and privacy. In particular, the deployment of such systems in public spaces, as well as our workplaces and homes, reconfigures common understandings and experiences of what it means to have no expectation of privacy. Although in principle we are not supposed to expect to be anonymous in public, prior to the uptake of FRT we knew that in many cases we were. If nothing else, human memory and recognition can be fallible and ephemeral. In contrast, automated facial identification introduces the prospect of a world in which machines can dramatically surpass human recognition and recall, making it possible, in theory, to track everyone at all times. If US soldiers can run live face detection in the mountain regions of Afghanistan, there is little reason to feel that similar monitoring could not take place in Amsterdam or Austin.

The examples outlined so far in this chapter raise concerns over what consequences such a transformation of public and private space might have for personal privacy and individual autonomy. Key here are concerns over likely erosions of trust and their displacement by technologies of monitoring and surveillance. The forms of trust that have traditionally enabled societies to function have relied on the preservation of spaces and times that were sheltered from the forms of surveillance and control enabled by the widespread implementation of automated recognition and tracking. Such conditions are altered significantly with the widespread deployment of systems that can generate automated responses to 'suspicious' individuals when a face is linked to a criminal profile, or when it is interpreted as showing signs of 'malintent', 'hostility' or simply not being 'known'. Errors in these calculations, of course, can have dire consequences. A surveillance system that erroneously identifies someone as a dangerous individual might result in a more aggressive or violent response by the authorities – and this risk might be systematically elevated for people of colour because of existing biases. It is not a coincidence that US news reports of wrongful arrests on the basis of facial recognition during the past ten years or so have almost always featured the wrongful arrest of Black men.

In one sense, as Nora Khan (2019) observes, a major concern in an age of facial recognition is not the act of being watched but the act of being watched *badly* – i.e. not being fully or properly known by machines that are designed to know just enough to fulfil their narrow-defined purpose. Arguably, people in many countries had already become inured to being tracked, watched and surveilled long before the implementation of FRT. Yet we are only beginning to become concerned by the blunt ways that the results of recent forms of surveillance are playing out. As Khan puts it, this relates to the dangers 'of an imprecise logic, a high probability of misalignment of what is seen, what is named, and what is then "known" by this eye, that connects to a digital brain that is trying valiantly to know just *enough* to maximize profit'. As she continues, 'Being badly watched, then, becomes secondary to being badly named because of that watching. Machines can see us both very clearly and very incorrectly, such that the incorrect or incomplete tagging is frozen into an objective, lasting state of knowing who we are, the kind of people we are likely to be.'

Of course, any instances of misrecognition will often be of minor consequence for the institutions involved in making these identifications, yet they can be devastating for the individuals who have been wronged. For example, the deployment of facial recognition software with a 99.9 per cent success rate to ensure that only eligible people access unemployment benefits across the United States nevertheless resulted in thousands of vulnerable claimants having to go without essential payments for weeks, and therefore struggling to make ends meet (Feathers 2021). For mass-scale programs such as India's Aadhaar national biometrics identification infrastructure, Ranjit Singh (2019: 501) notes that 'a 1 percent error rate in digital services used by all Indians translates into challenges faced by approximately 13 million people.'

One of the most chilling recent examples of mass harms associated with FRT involved US military use of biometrics. In 2021, as the US military forces hastily abandoned their 20-year occupation of Afghanistan, it quickly became feared that the large-scale biometric datasets collected by the United States on millions of Afghan police and army personnel would fall into the hands of the incoming Taliban regime. Set up by US forces to combat pay-cheque fraud, this dataset of iris scans, fingerprints and facial images potentially gave the Taliban the capacity to quickly identify Afghans who had worked in support of United States and other western forces (Guo and Noor 2021). While it was reckoned that the abandoned Handheld Interagency Identity Detection Equipment and datasets only gave limited access to the biometric data, the incident sparked fears over the security of such data, and how the utility of facial recognition can dramatically shift depending on who is using it and with what intentions. In a conflict situation or fragile political context, the idea of FRT falling into enemy hands is hardly an 'unexpected consequence'.

The fate of this biometric archive highlights the issues raised by the portability of the database. If, as Sekula (1986: 16) has argued, the central artefact of earlier photographic identification systems was 'not [the] camera but the filing cabinet', then the central artefact of automated facial recognition is the database, which has its own distinctive characteristics. Digital databases are more portable and far more easily (and less transparently) duplicated than physical archives of photographs. At the same time, they are more tightly bound to individual bodies. These combined attributes contribute to both the way facial databases are created and how they can be circulated. Thus, for example, a company like Clearview AI is able to covertly amass what is reportedly one of the largest facial identity databases by simply scraping images publicly available online. This method of archive production means we are not necessarily aware of how and when we are incorporated into the archive. By the same token, those who control the archive are not necessarily aware when it has been compromised, copied and shared. Once compromised, as concerns about the US military databases in Afghanistan highlight, it is prohibitively difficult to disassociate oneself from the database. One might be able to forge or dissimulate other identity credentials, such as ID cards, but not so easily one's face or fingerprints. On the one hand, then, the database as archive is relatively 'lighter' than its filing cabinet precursor – a set of files that would have filled the library of Congress can be copied and transferred in a matter of minutes. On the other hand, it is more firmly attached to its referents – who find it much more difficult to lose, conceal or alter the credentials that link them to the archive.

Some of the other examples in this chapter highlight the low-level attritions, inconveniences, incursions and interruptions that can result from the background use of FRT in social contexts. Telling here is how these 'micro-oppressions' are disproportionately experienced by those groups that are already vulnerable. For example, the use of FRT to identify prison visitors is likely to impact most on inmates' families legitimately wanting to visit their loved ones – adding an additional burden to visitation in the form of what Silkie Carlo (2019) describes as the unwarranted surveillance of biometric scanning. If prison authorities want to make prison visits even more stressful and unappealing, then adding facial recognition scanning is a good place to start.

Indeed, some of the examples in this chapter point to the often subtle, context-dependent ways that any FRT application can be experienced as harmful. Take, for example, Uber's Real-Time Check ID process. As described earlier, since 2016 Uber drivers in some regions have been sometimes subjected to a Real-Time Check ID process. This involves the Uber driver app asking the driver to pose for a photograph which is then matched against their official driver profile photo. The driver is prohibited from logging on to the Uber platform and starting work until their photo is verified. This feature is triggered by Uber's behavioural data and algorithmic modelling flagging the driver for potentially fraudulent activity, such as allowing an unauthorized person to work under the same account. Ultimately, then, the ways in which this simple facial recognition feature is being deployed and engaged with are shaped by the wider context of working for Uber and the limited extent to which Uber is prepared to trust its drivers. For many private car owners, the option of having facial verification is seen as a desirable additional feature – an example of what Chris Gilliard (2020) has termed 'luxury surveillance'. This same logic is very different to the experience of having to pass an externally imposed test before being allowed to drive a car to start one's shift as a precariously employed Uber driver.

Therefore, we need to pay close attention to the consequences of being watched badly and watched oppressively for specific groups and populations. Indeed, all these examples need to be seen in light of the long-standing concern about the impact of racial and gender bias evidenced by existing facial recognition systems (Browne 2015; Buolamwini and Gebru 2018; Introna and Wood 2004). This relates back to recurring findings discussed in previous chapters of greater error rates for women and people of colour. When fed into systems for security screening, commerce and law enforcement, such errors can lead to forms of discrimination, exclusion and violence that affect people's life chances. At the same time, these examples highlight the potential of abuse of personal information gathered from facial recognition systems since these systems do not simply identify people but gather information about their movements and actions throughout the course of the day. As Atanasoski and Vora (2019: 127) argue, the automation of vision associated with the deployment of always-on smart cameras results in a reconfiguration of perception premised on the prospect of capturing as much data as possible in real time – what they see as attempting to reach a state of 'persistent surveillance' and 'permanent watch' with the attempt to 'totalize perspectives through an aggregation of images'.

By allowing individuals to be identified across different cameras as they move through physical space, facial recognition therefore enables the detection of additional biometric patterns – not just of one's face but of the rhythm and shape of one's movements and activities throughout the course of the day. This information can reveal protected categories of information (regarding medical conditions, for example) and other details of people's intimate and personal lives, transforming public safety systems into powerful tools for authoritarian regimes of control, or tools for personal abuses, stalking and similar. In other words, the possibility of digital biometric identification should not be understood in narrow terms as the natural outgrowth of technical advancements in identification systems. Instead, these technologies are being envisioned and designed to fulfil certain perceived social necessities and political–economic demands of large-scale, late capitalist societies – societies characterized by a predominance of mediated forms of social organization and vastly asymmetrical distributions of wealth. The expansion of computer networks has created new problems of communication-without-bodies, necessitating new techniques for identifying people, verifying their legitimate identities and otherwise gaining knowledge about who they are.

All these erosions of privacy are not to be taken lightly. As Jeffrey Rosen (2011: 216) argues, 'privacy is necessary . . . to protect important social relationships – to make it possible for people to interact as citizens in the public square, as professionals in the workplace, and as friends, lovers, and family members in intimate group settings.' In short, privacy is inseparable from a baseline sense of autonomy, and autonomy is a crucial ingredient of democratic citizenship and legitimation. One of the hazards of the deployment of comprehensive systems of FRT surveillance is that they undermine autonomy and displace trust – developments that, in turn, threaten the forms of responsibility upon which both freedom and democracy rely. In a society in which one is monitored all the time, it becomes difficult to differentiate between behaving because one wants to or because one is compelled to. In a society in which everyone is watched all the time, the default setting is a lack of trust – why else would it be necessary to treat everyone as though they might be a possible suspect? On a practical level, there is no such thing as perfect surveillance – however, there is a point at which it becomes so comprehensive that it shrinks the space for autonomy and (falsely) promises to dispense with trust.

Questioning the reasons behind 'problematic' facial recognition

While these latter points might seem serious to some, other readers might still be questioning the extent to which these 'concerning' iterations of FRT should actually be considered to be of significant concern. For example, defenders of police use of facial recognition for identifying otherwise unknown suspects might argue that we have always had witness misidentification – often leading to grievous miscarriages of justice. There have always been racist police officers and racially motivated misdemeanours and malpractice within police forces. It could be reasoned that there is nothing substantially new about the problems associated with use of facial recognition in policing. Any concerns with police facial recognition perhaps relate to the nature of policing rather than specific problems with the technology. Similar counter-arguments might be raised in support of the other forms of FRT discussed in this chapter – from oppressive regimes through to the authoritarian nature of prisons or the prevalence of neighbourhood vigilantism and domestic abuse. In all these cases, issues with FRT piggyback on wider concerns and long-standing societal problems.

Criticism of the particular forms of FRT highlighted in this chapter relate to wider opposition to the structures and systems that FRT is being used to support. For example, anyone opposed to military intervention (if not military conflict altogether) is going to oppose the military use of any technology on a battlefield. Anyone concerned with the militarization of police forces and supportive of calls to 'defund the police' is going to be concerned about police misuse of all forms of surveillance technology. Concerns over the use of FRT in prisons is likely to stem from broader concerns over growing imprisonment of young males of colour and the increasing oppressive and inhumane conditions of prisons. FRT might well be indicative of these wider concerns but it is not the sole problem. This line of reasoning is often picked up by proponents for the increased use of FRT who argue, along with Commissioner O'Neill, that twenty-first-century technology is necessary to police a twenty-first-century city. Facial recognition is clearly powerful in terms of its speed, scope and scale. Following this logic, many people are understandably unwilling to give up on the benefits of this technology, both imagined and real. Who does not want to live in a society where it is easier for law enforcement to identify and track down legitimate suspects? For example, reporting by the *New York Times* provided several police accounts of the ease with which officers' unofficial use of Clearview AI allowed them to identify suspects who might otherwise have evaded justice indefinitely. Many people might well conclude that these beneficial ends justify the alarming means.

These are difficult arguments to refute. This technology is clearly not perfect, but neither are existing alternative ways of doing things. Moreover, presuming that we accept the need for countries to have armed forces, imprison offenders and maintain secure borders, then it is necessary to develop reliable forms of identification in these contexts. FRT might not be perfect but many people are prepared to accept that the advantages outweigh any inconveniences and occasional missteps with the caveat that this is technology that needs to be used with caution and effective human oversight. For example, police should clearly only be using FRT for providing initial leads (rather than for arresting suspects simply based on the machine's results), which can then be followed up by traditional detective work. Most of the mis-arrests noted earlier could be seen to have resulted from defective policing rather than defective technology. Moreover, it could be argued that any technical problems are likely to be solvable in the near future. In this sense, many people remain willing to countenance some form of FRT use by police, security and other agencies. From this perspective, the pressing question is how to ensure that these uses of facial recognition are subject to rigorous forms of transparency and public accountability.

Arguments that facial recognition can be 'fixed' and made 'fairer'

We will return to these arguments across the remainder of the book. For the time being, it is worth concentrating on one element of this defence of FRT – the idea that any harms of misidentification associated with the technology can be resolved technically through the more extensive development of data science approaches. For sure, there is little that FRT developers can do about rogue police officers and oppressive military juntas. However, there is growing belief that the serious problems of bias and discrimination can be addressed. Here we focus on the criticisms of FRT relating to race – notably, the issue that this is technology that does not technically 'work' in terms of recognizing people of colour, and that it is also associated with a range of racially directed forms of discrimination, oppression and harms.

These criticisms align with the wider Black Lives Matter protests in 2020 that kick-started a number of high-profile facial recognition bans across the United States and continue to sustain considerable doubts about the technology in the minds of policy makers and executives around the world. Indeed, the issue of race continues to be a major stumbling block faced by facial recognition developers, and a topic of much contention and argument. However, as far as many computer scientists and technology actors are concerned, these are issues that are solvable – a teething problem that will soon be resolved. As a headline in *Wired* magazine put it bluntly, 'Should We Teach Facial Recognition Technology About Race?' (Chen 2017). This logic is certainly worth pursuing in a little more detail. Are the racial harms of FRT fixable? If so, what does this tell us about the long-term viability of this technology?

Technical concerns about racial bias in FRT often relate to the provenance of the large datasets of photographs used to train facial recognition algorithms. Given their centrality to the whole FRT project, it is important to pay close attention to how training datasets are compiled and used. Traditionally, these datasets are seen as lying at the heart of any problem with representativeness and bias in how FRTs can 'recognize' some individuals better than others – especially in terms of racial discrimination. As noted in previous chapters, many critics contend that such biases underpin the trend for FRT systems to have difficulty engaging with faces that are not featured prominently in these key datasets. An FRT trained on a mass of photos that does not contain sufficient numbers of a specific racial or age group might well have difficulty 'recognizing' people with similar characteristics. As we saw in chapter 2, this leads to the popular notion that any misrecognition or 'discrimination' can be fixed through the creation of more representative and inclusive datasets. As Stevens and Keyes (2021) put it, 'enrol[ling] more Black and brown faces into facial recognition datasets – with the intent of making systems "work" for marginalized populations'.

However, these well-intentioned efforts (such as FairFace and Diversity in Faces outlined in chapter 2) highlight the extreme difficulty of fixing issues of bias and discrimination within even the largest and diverse datasets. As has been pointed out by numerous commenters, recent 'de-biasing' efforts to diversify the facial recognition training dataset illustrate the wide (and perhaps fundamental) gulf that exists between computer science and social science conceptions of the 'problem' of FRT. Efforts such as FairFace and Diversity in Faces are therefore seen as flawed along a number of lines. First is indignation about the sourcing of images and the overriding of concerns about a lack of regard for consent for inclusion, which results in a dehumanizing process that ensures that the subject of the photograph has no right to speak back about how they are described (Stevens and Keyes 2021). This alone has been termed facial recognition's 'dirty little secret' (Solon 2019).

Secondly, there is the questionable attribution of labels to photographic images of faces. As noted in chapter 2, photographic datasets used to train and test facial recognition models and algorithms are based on labels that provide 'ground truth' from which the system results can be compared and tested. This raises a number of issues – first in terms of the choice of which labels are used. For example, in simple statistical terms of validity, the decision to restrict gender to a finite number of categories (usually 'male' or 'female') flies in the face of the emerging understanding of gender as a fluid spectrum rather than as a list of fixed categories. This is also the case with labelling of racial attributes. For example, the FairFace algorithm makes the claim to be able to distinguish whether an individual is 'Black', 'white' or 'Latino' – the latter being a term to describe people in the United States with cultural ties to Latin America. Besides the issue that 'Latino' is not a racial category (Latinx people can be from any race), it is also impossible to detect from facial features. In the US context, for example, there are significant differences between Hispanic and Latinx ethnicities.

Even if we agree on the labels to be used, the process of inferring characteristics from photos alone is highly questionable. Indeed, the idea that machines (or humans) can correctly identify someone's 'race' from a photograph is flawed, as is the decision to rehabilitate debunked categories of racial distinctions. We live in times when race is widely understood to be a social construction rather than a biological trait. The decision to biologize race by taking skin colour (or any other facial feature) as a proxy indicator for an individual's race is a political one. It is also a very poor statistical one, given the wide variations in how people of one race might appear visually. In short, 'detecting' someone's race or ethnicity from their appearance risks descending into the murky (and discredited) world of physiognomy that amounts to little more than a misguided overreach of the technology.

Worse still, the Diversity in Faces research team eschewed any human labelling process altogether, instead choosing to use pre-existing computer vision tools. For example, to categorize skin colour and craniofacial structure, they used automated, algorithmic tools – systems designed for colour determination and structure selection. This form of categorization is both reductive and far removed from 'detecting' any sense of racial background or ethnic affiliation. Even with the best of intentions, the idea of 'fixing' FRT highlights a propensity for computer scientists and software developers to wade into complex and controversial social domains – not knowing (or caring) enough about the social contexts they are addressing. All told, there is little here to commend or even make good sense of. Perhaps the most pressing question is why FRT designers continue to pursue this line of work. As Sasha Costandza-Chock (2021) concludes, 'On a meta level, why is it that people think that it makes sense to make or assess a system by which a computer evaluates X without spending even the smallest amount of effort understanding X first?'

As Costandza-Chock implies, there is a recurring computational hubris in the attempt to parlay successes in statistical modelling from long-standing technical problems to addressing social issues that have deep and complex histories. This is easily discernible in realms where unexamined assumptions about race and ethnicity are baked into systems whose developers are equipped to think about technical challenges but less equipped (if not less inclined) to think about social ones.

Recognizing the difference between statistical bias and social harms

These concerns point to a fundamental mismatch between the ways in which computer scientists and social scientists approach the issue of 'bias'. The idea that FRT can be 'fixed' by better data practices and technical rigour conveys a particular mindset – i.e. that algorithms and AI models are not biased in and of themselves. Instead, algorithms and AI models simply amplify bias that might have crept into the datasets that they are trained in and/or the data that they are fed. As such, it might appear that any data-driven bias is ultimately fixable with better data.

Nevertheless, as Deb Raji (2021) describes, this is not the case. Of course, it is right to acknowledge that the initial generation of data can reflect historical bias, and that the datasets used to develop algorithmic models will often contain representation and measurement bias. However, every aspect of an algorithmic system is a result of programming and design decisions and can therefore contain additional biases. These include decisions about how tasks are conceived and codified, as well as how choices are modelled. In particular, algorithmic models are also subject to what are termed aggregation biases and evaluation biases. All told, any outcome of an algorithmic model is shaped by subjective human judgements, interpretations and discretionary decisions along the way. In this sense, many critics argue that FRT developers are best advised to focus on increasing the diversity of their research and development teams, rather than merely the diversity of their training datasets.

But this is not the end of the story. For many social scientists, the key message from most of the examples raised in this chapter is inexorably linked to how the algorithmic outputs and predictions of FRTs are then used – by, for example racist police officers, abusive spouses and suspicious employers. Ultimately, concerns over the bias and discriminations of FRT relate to the harms that an FRT system can do. As many of the examples outlined in the chapter suggest, there are a lot of harms that are initiated and amplified through the use of FRT. While many of these are existing harms, the bottom line remains that FRT used in a biased society will result in biased outcomes that will then result in increased harms. Thus, as Alex Allbright (2019) puts it, rather than focusing on the biases of predictive tools in isolation, we also need to consider how they are used in different contexts – not least social settings and institutional systems that are 'chock-full' of human judgements, human discretions and human biases.

So all of the harms of FRT discussed so far in this book need to be seen in terms of biased datasets, biased models *and* the biased contexts and uneven social relations within which any algorithmic system is used. This means that algorithmic 'bias' is not simply a technical data problem, but a sociotechnical problem of humans and data . . . and therefore not something that can ever be 'fixed'. Humans will always act in subjective ways; our societies will always be unequal and discriminatory. As such, our data-driven tools will inevitably be at least as flawed as the worldviews of the people who make them and use them. Moreover, our data-driven tools are most likely to amplify existing differences and unfairness, unless they are deliberately designed to be biased towards more inclusive outcomes and positive discrimination. Either way, there cannot be a completely objective, neutral and value-free facial recognition system – our societies and our technologies simply do not work along such lines.

The danger, of course, is not that FRT will reproduce existing biases and inequalities but that, as an efficient and powerful tool, it will exacerbate them. The development of a more effective or accurate means of oppression is not one to be welcomed. Instead, many applications of FRT can be accused of bolstering what Ruha Benjamin (2019) terms 'engineered inequality' by leading to injustices and disadvantage, given their design and implementation 'in a society structured by interlocking forms of domination'. Thus, as far as Benjamin is concerned, applying more inclusive datasets 'is not a straightforward good but is often a form of unwanted exposure' (2019: 125).

Against this background, it seems reasonable to suggest that much of the tension between computer scientists eager to fix FRT and critics who are incandescent about inherent harms comes down to profound differences in terminology and perceptions of the object of concern. Deborah Raji reminds us that computer scientists, technologists and data scientists often still take offence when confronted with talk of 'algorithmic bias' because of differences in terminology. In technical data terms, people are often trained to think about bias in very precise terms of statistical bias – one of the data issues that any AI scientist will strive to minimize when developing accurate algorithms and machine learning models. As Kate Crawford (2017) puts it, 'we are speaking different languages when we talk about bias'. To avoid such confusion, talk of social 'bias' is perhaps better framed as unfairness, harm and discrimination. In computer science terms, these conversations are perhaps best understood as a problem with classification, and the classifications that technology developers ascribe to people and their social contexts. In other words, addressing issues of statistical bias, under-representation and variance in datasets is not the main problem to be confronted. To think that we can address these issues through 'better' datasets or more efficient systems is the ultimate case of technological essentialism and data solutionism.

Conclusions

The social problems associated with FRT reach far beyond any technical concerns with statistical basis, under-representative datasets and other facets of the computer and data science that underpin the technology. Instead, the harms of FRT are entwined with the societies in which they are deployed. Raising these issues does not mean denying the obvious benefits (and possible 'goods') associated with some incarnations of FRT. As we saw in chapter 4, many people experience FRT as a source of convenience and safety. Yet, as has just been explored in the current chapter, this is clearly not the case for all people. Some of the instances discussed in this chapter constitute genuine sustained threats to people's liberty, human rights and freedoms. These are not outcomes that can be easily dismissed. The case against the widespread use of FRT in society remains compelling, and not easily resolved.

It is also important to recognize the breadth of these problematic uses. In this chapter, we have focused primarily on a few countries – notably the United States, China and Russia. Yet these countries are not outliers. Countries all around the world support the use of FRT by their police forces, armies, border guards and prisons. China's deployment of FRT against the Muslim ethnic minority is

not an isolated case – oppressive regimes operate all around
the world in a variety of guises. For example, Indigenous
rights campaigners argue that it is not coincidental that
the early adoption of FRT by Australian police occurred in
regions with high proportions of Aboriginal populations.
Elsewhere, one of the great fears surrounding the roll-out
of India's national biometric Aadhaar program is the similar
use of FRT to 'detect' and enforce caste frameworks – thus
exacerbating what anti-caste activists have termed 'digital
Brahmanism'. As Amba Kak (cited in Dixit 2019) puts it,
'Can you use facial recognition to detect things like caste or
religion? Given the [polarized] political situation in India,
that would be our dystopia.'

So, regardless of national context, the continued roll-out
of FRT needs to be seen as deeply problematic. That said, the
last two chapters have shown that these issues are complex
and often contradictory. There are clearly a diverse set of
uses, justifications and perspectives on the implementation
of FRT in society. Some applications of FRT could be seen
as heart-warming – families being reunited, lost pets being
found. Many of the applications in chapter 4 are simply
convenient features of everyday life – momentary transactions and checks that we quickly stop noticing – doors
opening, phones being unlocked, payments being made. Yet,
as this chapter has shown, FRT also anticipates a fundamental reconfiguration of everyday life with profound social
consequences. The question of how FRT continues to be
developed and applied in our societies is a serious one. This
is both a technical question of what works (and adds value)
and also a moral question of what goes wrong and ultimately
harms our society. These dilemmas are explored in the next
chapter. Even if most readers of this book may not yet have
encountered all these different forms of FRT in their own
daily lives, how might things pan out in the near future?
What would our lives be like in an FRT-saturated society?
What might we be letting ourselves in for?

6

Facial Futures: Emerging Promises and Possible Perils

Introduction

While the last two chapters have highlighted a wide range of current uses of facial recognition technology, we are still in the relatively early stages of its implementation. Most shopping malls, schools and prisons are yet to see the installation of facial recognition systems and services. There are many familiar ways of paying for your morning coffee or checking on visitors to your front door that do not involve face scanning. Thus many of the facial recognition applications we have discussed remain niche and yet to be taken up in great numbers. To date, the main areas where FRT is beginning to be taken up at scale are controlled and security-intense contexts – such as airports, border crossings and casinos. While the foundations have been put into place over the past few years, we are a long way off living in a facial recognition society.

Nevertheless, the industry envisions avenues for the profitable widespread roll-out of the technology as it becomes cheaper and more powerful in coming years, and many commentators see the increased adoption and use of FRT as inevitable. Such predictions are further bolstered by the ways in which facial recognition technologies fit neatly into the pattern of increasingly comprehensive and ubiquitous monitoring ushered in by the digital networked era and its surveillance-based economic model. Networked interactive devices capable of capturing a growing range of information have been deployed widely in the name of customization, risk management and greater efficiency. Facial recognition technology promises to make this data collection more complete and comprehensive. If nothing else, the expectation of over a billion smartphones being unlocked by their users' faces suggests that this is not technology that is going to go away soon. Given the tremendous investment in the technology's development, it is worth paying attention to the expectations and predictions that surround the continued development and deployment of this technology over the next decade or so.

This chapter takes a forward-looking approach to exploring some of the anticipated uses of facial recognition technology and the attendant social consequences of these uses. In particular, we consider how the logics already apparent in the existing iterations of facial recognition described so far in the book might play out further. Are countries around the world headed towards some version of a Chinese social credit system in which facial recognition serves as the entry point to multiple databases that can be used for everything from permitting travel to providing credit? How will facial recognition be articulated to systems designed to 'read' and 'infer' further information about the people who come under their gaze – from an individual's trustworthiness to their susceptibility to targeted forms of customized messaging and manipulation? How will automated systems connected to smart cameras reconfigure users' access to physical spaces of labour, leisure and domesticity?

This is not an exercise in fantastical thinking or sci-fi dystopia. Some of these imagined uses of FRT simply presume the continued take-up of already existing technology. Yet it is also worth exploring some of the more speculative applications of facial recognition technology that align with (and have potential to exacerbate) existing tendencies and priorities. Not everything that we are writing in this chapter will hold up to scrutiny when read ten years later . . . but it is likely that some of it will. Even speculative uses that do *not* eventually come to fruition nevertheless can tell us much about the imperatives driving the current development of the technology. Even if these applications turn out to be dead ends, the priorities they serve are likely to continue to shape the future of surveillance and monitoring technologies and practices.

Anticipating a future when your face becomes metadata

In one sense, it is possible to anticipate a relatively straightforward and all-encompassing near future – characterized by total surveillance, where our faces become prime sources of personal information. Indeed, one of the themes that have emerged across previous chapters is the way in which facial recognition systems can turn faces into metadata. In other words, our faces can be used as a source of information about our activities and interactions that make it possible to identify, link, sort and respond to them. This transformation promises, in many cases, efficiency and convenience for the person whose face is being 'recognized' – potentially displacing the need for keys, wallets, ID cards and all the other bits and pieces we carry around with us to prove our identity and ensure right of access. Furthermore, this application of FRT offers to be a key component in realizing the futuristic scenario of 'smart spaces' and the promise of environments that can recognize and mould themselves to the people who are passing through. Indeed, one of the key promises of 'ubiquitous' computing is that any space can learn about those who pass through it in order to customize their experience – whether through providing bespoke messaging, playing their favourite music, or responding automatically to their food preferences.

By the same token, such spaces can also be used to sort individuals and deny access, detaining or excluding someone if they are deemed to be in violation of rules or regulations. In digitally enhanced spaces, the promise of recognition is not simply to make an impression but also to generate a response. A space that recognizes you can open a door for you, and then pay for your purchases (out of your own bank account) without you having to swipe or scan. It can show you ads that are tailored to your preferences, allow access to public transport without you having to produce a transit card, or enable you to start your car without a key fob. It can ensure that you, and only you, receive the entitlements you are owed, and it can confirm your identity even when you lose your passport. Your proof of identification is always with you and cannot be lost or stolen. In short, these are software-augmented environments which use your face to ease access, interaction and transaction while protecting your possessions.

The flip side of this promised convenience, of course, is the eclipse of forms of privacy to which we have grown accustomed and that provide some sense of social 'wiggle room' and personal autonomy. Many of the forms of convenience enabled by facial recognition rely on pervasive monitoring that could easily exacerbate oppressive social control, especially for those individuals already subject to oppression. Indeed, up until recently, we may have had the sense that many of the activities we engage in throughout the course of our day allow us to retain some sense of anonymity, despite the networked devices we carry with us. When we glance in a shop window, flip through a book on the shelf of a bookstore or meet up with a friend at a café, we do not expect that these activities will be captured and linked to us. The addition of a recognitive capability to the surveillance cameras that permeate a growing range of spaces, however, tags our activities with our identity, and thus makes these activities legible in new ways. As outlined in chapter 5, the COVID-19 pandemic saw companies avail themselves of facial recognition technology to monitor whether employees were respecting social distancing guidelines. However, the continued post-pandemic use of this technology could also keep track of how much time employees spend chatting with one another or perhaps, more pointedly, who is speaking to workers attempting to organize the shop floor.

This is what it means to describe facial recognition technology as a form of metadata collection – technology that promises to add extra content and identifying information to the images captured by the almost one billion surveillance cameras in operation globally. Add to those cameras the prospect of every smartphone being equipped with a facial recognition app that can be applied to any photo it captures, and the result is an increasingly comprehensive form of individual tracking. Such a system would be further enhanced by the prospect of so-called 'augmented reality', which envisions the addition of an interactive layer of digital technology superimposed on physical reality. In an augmented reality world (for example, some form of Facebook's recently touted 'metaverse'), someone wearing smart glasses could receive targeted information about spaces through which they moved – everything from historical information of interest to customized advertising and personal messages left by friends. As the tech guru and digital futurist Kevin Kelly (2019) has observed, making augmented reality operational would require 'a planet full of cameras that are always on'. Equipped with facial recognition, such cameras would eliminate anonymity entirely.

If our faces come to provide identifying metadata about people (similar to the way that licence plates identify individual vehicles), then it is likely that highly personal information will be captured by those who control the smart-camera networks. For example, details of where we travel throughout the course of the day can reveal all kinds of sensitive information about our intimate, political and professional lives (Mayer 2013). Tracking visits to particular doctors' offices, may, for example, reveal information about medical conditions. Information about where we shop or eat, or how often we exercise, could provide information about general levels of fitness. Information about whom we meet with, where we go, and which public events we attend can provide insight into our political alignments and affiliations, as well as our social networks. Moreover, the prospect of comprehensive monitoring promises to concentrate informational power offline as it did online. Platforms that monitor and track individuals based on facial recognition technology will be able to create detailed profiles that will be of use across the realms of marketing, health care and employment. A world that is fully equipped with facial recognition technology promises to be a total surveillance society, which is why critics are moving quickly to argue for the regulation – if not total cessation – of how this technology continues to be developed.

Looking beyond total surveillance: scenarios of verification, identification and inference

Of course, if we are judicious in our use of the technology and deploy it in accordance with overarching commitments to human and civil rights, we may avoid this fate of total surveillance. However, recent history suggests this is a very big 'if'. The lure of new markets for technological 'innovations' combined with the goals of increased control, convenience, and efficiency has tended to be a primary driver of technological development in the digital media realm. With this tendency in mind, there are a number of more specific ways that we now might go to extrapolate from the existing deployment of the technology to what different futures characterized by the widespread implementation of facial recognition technology might look like. In particular, we can explore three distinct (but related) application domains for the future development of facial recognition technology: verification, identification and inference.

Verification, as we have discussed in previous chapters, refers to processes of one-to-one matching for securing transactions and interactions. For example, an automated teller machine might use facial recognition to verify that you are really the person entering the passcode for your bank account, or that the credit card you used really belongs to you. The familiar contemporary example is that of border control, where facial recognition technology is used to verify that the person presenting your passport is really you. *Identification* refers to the one-to-many searches used by police and others to determine the identity of unknown individuals. In the case of the casino, for example, such a system could match the faces of entrants to a database of problem gamblers, or perhaps VIP 'high rollers'. A supermarket might use facial recognition to determine whether entering customers are convicted shoplifters. *Inference*, on the other hand, refers to the forms of physiognomic detection discussed in previous chapters – divining additional information beyond identification, such as ethnicity, age, gender, or even character traits and emotional states. This latter category, as we shall see, anticipates a host of potential uses that range from potentially helpful to profoundly dystopian, such as the attempt to read criminal disposition from an individual's face.

The degree to which these different logics play out in the future application of FRT depends on who has access to the technology and the regulations that govern its use. Experience suggests that much of the technology will be in the control of commercial entities that value profit over civil rights commitments, justice and democracy. One of the recurring pitfalls of technological futurism is the temptation to envision technical advances in the abstract: 'Wouldn't it be great if we could create a system that could diagnose serious medical conditions just by scanning someone's face?' Of course, if technically possible, this would be a welcome development if the technology were used to assist in early intervention that saved lives (Zharovskikh 2020). But what if this technology were developed by a commercial organization that sold it to private health insurers to enable them to turn down applications for insurance cover for those who might be showing signs of costly illnesses? Or, by the same token, what if this technology were used to screen potential employees in order to weed out those who might become unable to work at a later date?

As these more pointed scenarios illustrate, there is no sense in anticipating the future development of technology in the abstract – all such systems are deployed in social contexts that shape the uses to which they will be put. Therefore, it is reasonable to expect that the development of facial technologies by commercial companies will seek out the most profitable applications, and if these turn out to be warning insurance companies about high-cost patients, then that is how the technology will be used. With this in mind, the following sections attempt to situate possible deployments of facial recognition technology within the political and economic relations that define contemporary society rather than simply imagining them in the abstract.

The social stratification of physical space

Drawing on the terminology of media history and regulation, we might describe the familiar, common-sense conception of public space as a medium of 'common carriage'. The general principle here is that everyone (except for those who have been deprived of their freedom) can move through public space equally, regardless of who they are. That is, the pavement does not make a distinction between me and a friend, neighbour or stranger who might also be walking along the same street. Public parks are meant to remain neutral with respect to those who pass through them, and public signalling systems, such as traffic lights and street signs, apply indiscriminately to all. In practice, of course, we know that public spaces like parks and streets are structured by relations of exclusion, meaning that different groups and individuals will have very different experiences of how accessible, welcoming or safe these spaces are. Even though public space is meant to be neutral with respect to those who use it, we know that it already discriminates (and has done so historically – as in the case of the segregation of access to public facilities such as pools, bathrooms, public libraries and so on). However, the ideal is meant to be one of general public access and use.

The fact that this ideal has never been obtained is about to be further called into question by the development of automated technologies that make it possible to identify and categorize individuals in real time as they move through public and shared spaces. As we have seen across previous chapters, sports stadia and entertainment venues envision the use of facial recognition for sorting crowds into more and less desirable customers – those VIP who are 'whitelisted' (in terminology that cannot help but invoke racial coding) and those 'blacklisted' as potential troublemakers (Hutchins and Andrejevic 2021). The goal is to use facial recognition to develop automated systems for channelling and regulating the movement of individuals. Data collection becomes linked to interventions in physical, lived space. Automated turnstiles, for example, could sort crowds at potential bottlenecks, speeding the entrance of VIPs and detaining 'undesirables'. The same principle could apply to a range of access and signalling technologies. The lift industry, for example, is developing buttonless technology that assigns people to particular floors based on their intended destination upon check-in. When linked to facial recognition technology, such systems would manage crowd flows more efficiently while also enabling more comprehensive forms of access control. Known individuals would automatically be routed to the appropriate floor, while unknowns would be blocked or detained for further identification.

There is, of course, a long history of stratifying movement through shared space. We might think of the geography of roads constructed by Israel in occupied Palestine to facilitate the mobility of Jewish residents while limiting that of Palestinians and fragmenting their territory (Weizman 2012). In the United States, it has been suggested that Robert Moses' bridges over the Long Island Expressway were constructed to be too low to allow buses to reach the city's showcase beaches, effectively rendering them inaccessible to inner-city residents without the economic means to purchase automobiles. These are relatively low-resolution forms of population channelling, dependent on inflexible infrastructures. Both examples recall Deleuze's (2007: 322) formulation of the road as a control mechanism: 'You do not confine people with a highway. But by making highways, you multiply the means of control . . . people can travel infinitely and "freely" without being confined while being perfectly controlled.' We might describe this form of control as secured mobility – differentiated from more static forms of control such as incarceration or immobilization.

Facial recognition technology, by contrast, offers the possibility of real-time customization of control. In this respect, it lends itself to dynamic forms of individuation and customization. It is perhaps telling, in this regard, that some IT companies are working on facial recognition systems for identifying faces through the windows of automobiles (Kopstein 2017). This would mark a shift in current forms of automated traffic monitoring which rely on licence plates. Whereas licence plate identification provides some wiggle room in terms of identification (as can be attested to by anyone who has ever received a traffic ticket for their car when someone else was driving), a face promises the prospect of unique identification. When connected to dynamic forms of mobility control (lifts, traffic lights, turnstiles and automatic doors), facial recognition makes it possible to engage in the governance of mobility at the individual level. Smart spaces and channels that incorporate facial recognition will thus make it possible to regulate and stratify mobility on an individual level. Those who are deemed to be VIPs, or who pay for the privilege, may find their way smoothed by roads and passages that provide them accelerated access, traffic lights that turn green for them, and special offers directed to them via augmented reality platforms. In other words, it may be the case that people in close proximity might nevertheless find themselves encountering completely different spaces in terms of the opportunities and access available to them. When a space recognizes the individuals it contains, it can be reconfigured to respond differently to different individuals.

The shadow of control

Many of the uses envisioned for facial recognition technology invoke the promise of efficiency, convenience, care and/or security. Nevertheless, as noted in the previous chapter, in each case this promise is shadowed by the spectre of control and exclusion. For example, it might seem convenient for an app to read your mood in order to customize your music playlist or film recommendations, but mood data could also be used to exclude you from a job opportunity or expose you to manipulative advertising during a vulnerable moment. Similarly, ubiquitous automated facial recognition might make it easier to capture and hold criminals accountable, but it might also be used to deter political speech and dissent. It is no coincidence that many of these alternative uses are what might be described as 'pre-emptive', drawing on monitoring technologies to facilitate action that might reduce future risk, harm or threat. This pattern is in keeping with the automation of surveillance (Andrejevic 2020), which relies on the collection and processing of large amounts of data to anticipate the future in ways that can be acted upon in the present. The goal of such forms of monitoring is not just to provide what might be described as a symbolic form of deterrence (as in the case of road signs that indicate speed cameras are in use), but to predict the activities of those who might not be deterred by such measures. Many of these uses are thus inferential in nature, linking identification with other attributes that might signal risk or threat.

There are various areas where such systems are likely to be deployed, as indicated by current industry trends. For example, in the realm of security, facial recognition forms part of what we introduced in chapter 2 as a 'surveillance assemblage'. In other words, FRT can be aligned with other monitoring technologies and data to assist in forms of threat detection and management. The California company FaceFirst, for example, claims to be able to combine facial recognition technology with data analytics to 'help you stop crimes before they start' (FaceFirst 2017: 2). This might include linking the identity of individuals to past instances of criminal behaviour, or even training 'smart' camera systems to detect patterns of behaviour that supposedly signify impending violence. The security start-up Athena claims to have developed cameras that have learned to detect when a fight is about to start (Tucker 2019). Facial recognition technology thus promises to address the question of how to link together data-driven forms of behaviour prediction with real-time forms of individual tracking – that is, to be able to identify who, at any given time in any given place, might pose a threat.

Similar systems are proposed that might use real-time biometric data (including facial expression, surface body temperature and heart rate) to discern 'malintent' and the intention to do harm in real time (Weinberger 2010). Such developments anticipate a future in which FRT can be used to detect and thwart potential offenders in real time, before any harmful action can be committed. In science fiction terms, this marks a *Minority Report* approach to crime in which the predictions of psychics are replaced with data mining, machine learning and facial detection. The ability to monitor individual-level activity and link it to a unique identity antici-pates a world in which everyone is assigned a dynamic 'risk assessment score' as they go through their daily lives. Each time we pass by a smart camera (and such cameras would be ubiquitous in this future scenario), our actions and expressions are parsed to see whether we might pose a threat in the moment.

The temporality of this type of risk assessment poses a challenge for assigning an appropriate response. If threats can be detected in real time, as they are about to emerge, how can the authorities keep up? Once automated detection becomes feasible, in other words, it opens up the need for automated response. A camera may detect that a fight is about to break out, but if there are no officials around to intervene then this is not much more useful than simply recording the fight to provide after-the-event evidence. Thus such systems push in the direction of automated forms of intervention envisioned by, for example, the equipping of drones with tasers, rubber bullets and more lethal weaponry. So-called smart spaces will likely do more than simply monitor – they will act directly on people in response to dynamic information supplied by embedded sensors. The result is reminiscent of another science fiction trope – the automated police officer able to detain and, if necessary, to respond with force (albeit with the added twist that their actions would be in response to anticipated transgression). Facial recognition has a key role to play in such developments because it links a particular individual with background forms of intelligence (patterns of online activity, social networks, tips from informers, past criminal activity and so on) and real-time biometric data (pulse rate, surface body temperature, facial expressions and more).

Such systems pose several potential threats to civil liberties and human rights. Much depends on how crime is defined by those who put powerful analytics and sensing technology to work. If, for example, political criticism and protest is criminalized, to the extent that such technologies are effective, they would pose a serious threat to freedom of thought and expression, as well as to democracy. As outlined in chapter 5,

FRT has already been used to identify and prosecute political protesters in Hong Kong, Moscow, Myanmar and elsewhere (Mozur 2019b). Moreover, the attempt to read and potentially criminalize one's inferred thoughts and intentions could constitute a violation of the doctrine of *forum internum* – the right of freedom of thought and conscience enshrined in the Universal Declaration of Human Rights (Petkoff 2012). It is hard to escape the conclusion that the development and deployment of such technologies would make it all too easy to threaten fundamental democratic freedoms and human rights. This does not necessarily mean, however, that people might not support their implementation in the name of enhanced public safety.

Social sorting for risk and opportunity

Of course, the logic of risk assessment and pre-emption is not limited to the realm of security and public safety, but is applicable to a wide range of other social interactions and transactions. For example, employers make risk assessments and behavioural predictions as a routine part of the hiring process, as do universities during the admissions process and health-care workers during patient intake and management. Here, then, we might anticipate a number of potential and anticipated uses of facial recognition across different social practices, many of which combine inferential and identificatory uses of the technology.

For example, in economic terms one of the primary spheres of risk is that of the extension of credit. Building on the promise that the face might provide some clue to inner intentions and tendencies, a Chinese company claims to have developed a system 'to analyse facial expressions of applicants to determine their willingness to repay the loans' (Gilmore 2017). Alternatively, in terms of health care, the face is a familiar locus for medical examination, which often features a preliminary examination of accessible interior parts via facial orifices: ear, nose and mouth. Facial recognition technology takes the model of the visage as the royal road to interiority a step further, anticipating the prospect of advanced diagnostics based on biometric sensors. Consider the example of Face2Gene, an app that claims to be able to diagnose genetic disorders through an automated analysis of facial features. Once again, we can discern the double-edged character of such forms of facial inference, raising the prospect of social sorting that could result in timely care and considerate response or in new forms of discrimination based on inferred medical conditions.

Interestingly, the ability to know people's bodies and minds via their faces is portrayed as a 'non-invasive' set of techniques because it does not require touching or manipulating the body. At the same time, however, it envisions turning people 'inside out' so that interior thoughts and feelings can be read directly from the body's surface. In this respect, it invokes what Rachel Hall (2007) has described as an 'aesthetics of transparency . . . motivated by the desire to turn the world (the body) inside out such that there would no longer be any secrets or interiors, human or geographical, in which our enemies (or the enemy within) might find refuge' (320–1). Indeed, for Magnet (2011), the defining failure of biometric technologies is their inability to deliver on the project of 'knowing' an individual via automated biometric sensors.

Suggestively, the mobilization of specification associated with biometric recognition embraces language borrowed from the lexicon of the surveillance economy: individual recognition and specification can enable custom-tailored treatment. The more data that can be collected (or so the story goes), the more accurate and effective the automated response is likely to be. Given that most medical treatment is personal, the implication is that interactions themselves may become automated: a medical 'bot' could provide customized responses via data-driven forms of patient screening. At the same time, the medical deployment of

FRT is a means of averting institutional risks. For example, by scanning the patient's face and checking it against the hospital database, the technology helps verify the person's identity and prevent fraud, such as 'someone impersonating a patient to get expensive medical treatment or drug dealers infiltrating hospitals' (Zharovskikh 2020). One and the same technology can assess medical conditions and secure medical facilities from fraud and threat. The logic repeats across a range of social practices. For example, when deployed in shopping centres, facial recognition can provide tailored customer experiences while also detecting possible shoplifters. In schools it can monitor attentiveness and check for suspicious activities. In sports stadia and casinos it can cater to VIPs and weed out troublemakers. The promised benefits oscillate between perceived risk and opportunity.

It is tempting to treat inferential uses of biometric monitoring, such as emotion and cognition detection, as highly speculative, unreliable and biased. Indeed, it is very hard to confirm whether emotion detection is accurate, and even people are often not able to reliably self-report their emotions and moods. However, the actual capacity of such systems, despite what they may promise, is not to gauge internal states but to match biometric data with subsequent outcomes. The goal, in other words, is not detailed analysis but shallow prediction. It is enough, for all practical purposes, that what gets judged as 'malintent' correlates with future criminal activity without having to determine whether an automated system has accurately assessed an individual's internal state in the moment. Indeed, the only 'proof' of interior access in such cases is external action. Unearthing reliable patterns of correlation relies in large part on the ability to train systems on large datasets. In order to be able to deliver on their promise, such systems pose the requirement of their widespread and general deployment. There is a vicious cycle at work here, with the promise of more accurate, efficient and useful systems reliant on the collection of more data. This accumulation of data, in turn, renders sense making impossible without the use of automated systems. As in the case of interactive media more generally, the entire system operates as a collection machine for amassing the huge amounts of data needed to feed the data mine and train machine learning systems.

Facial recognition and the 'integral accident'

Finally, it is always insightful when anticipating the possible futures of any technological innovation to consider worst-case scenarios. Many of the speculative uses of facial recognition described in this chapter run the risk of being completely inaccurate. There might well be little substance, for example, in the notion that creditworthiness might be read off the features or expressions of the face. Of course, the logic of data mining maintains that such correlations might always remain possible in the future, if only more data can be collected and analysed by more powerful computational methods.

Nevertheless, in many cases it remains impossible to tell whether the machine-generated outcomes are correct. For example, if someone is denied a job based on a series of micro-expressions, how can it be proved that this person might have been a model employee? The danger of such systems is that they can provide a convenient way of sorting through data fast enough to keep up with its accumulation, and that this convenience itself could become one of the main reasons for relying upon them. Barring some kind of obvious and persistent failure, testing these systems might come to seem prohibitively costly and time consuming. The real danger is perhaps not that the systems work as promised but that they come to be relied upon even without such proof. Who has gone back to check all the résumés that have been discarded by machines to see whether those people went on to success in the area for which they were deemed insuffi-ciently qualified? In some cases, the failures will be obvious

– as when a facial recognition system identifies an innocent person as a criminal suspect. Even in this case, the person might have to pay heavily in terms of time, reputation, inconvenience and lawyers' fees. However, in many cases the locus of the decision will be too opaque and the cost of challenging it too high to meaningfully and reliably contest it.

The tyranny of convenience may end up making FRT a keystone in the data-mining process, with facial recognition providing the universal ID that holds together this growing accumulation of data. The failure of this keystone anticipates a new type of accident – the automation of misidentification. The theorist Paul Virilio (2007 [1998]: 10) observed that every technological innovation is shadowed and defined by its characteristic accident: 'To invent the sailing ship or steamer is to invent the shipwreck. To invent the train is to invent the rail accident of derailment.' He subsequently updated this formulation for the information era, which he described as ushering in the era of the integral accident – in other words, one which 'causes other accidents in its wake'. Whereas industrial accidents were localized and particular (such as wrecks, crashes and leaks), Virilio reasoned that the advent of 'instantaneous transmissions brought about by telecommunications makes the accident global' (Virilio 2007 [1998]).

Seen in this light, there is much that might go wrong in terms of FRT, not least the global sense of paranoia associated with automated misidentification. Consider a future in which an individual's face comes to serve as a form of universal ID for legal, medical and financial purposes. In such a world, when one shows up to prove one's identity at the bank, the airport or the hospital, the recognition of other humans is discounted in comparison with the automated gaze of the system. Imagine, then, that the system malfunctions and leaves you denied credit, treatment, access, freedom because of a false match. This is a world in which the big 'Other' of the machine gaze goes awry – your car won't start, your phone will not let you log in. Imagine the prospect of automated false identifications. It might be, for example, that the legal violations and financial defaults of others are called up every time your face appears. At the same time, the documents you use to prove your identity need themselves to be identified by the very automated system that has misrecognized you. Unlike other credentials, biometrics cannot be easily replaced. If your password is compromised, you can change it, but if your retinal scan or face image become compromised, you cannot get new eyeballs or facial features (without major surgery). Such, perhaps, are the perils of the displacement of social forms of identification and verification onto the automated system, and the replacement of face-to-face interactions by the interface.

Conclusions

This is an extreme note on which to conclude, especially in light of the seemingly mundane and innocuous uses of FRT that have been presented earlier on in the book. Many of the future applications just outlined are speculative (although the speculations reflect tendencies that emerge from the industry literature) and do not (yet) accompany the relatively mundane and narrow uses of current facial recognition technology. Some of these descriptions need to be seen as social 'fictions' rather than social facts. Yet, as with all storytelling, these near-future visions of facial recognition foreground important issues, concerns, hopes and fears that we can take forward into the final chapter, where we attempt to make sense of what FRT is, and where we might want FRT to be heading.

As in the case of other recent technological developments, the framing of facial recognition in official and industry contexts tends to focus on perceived benefits without reflecting on the heightened surveillance and concentration of control with which these are associated. As we have learned from our experience with the World Wide Web and the forms of commercial and state surveillance it has enabled, it is important to consider the potential social harms that lurk behind the enthusiasm for the adoption of new technologies. The stories in this chapter offer a distinctly different take on facial recognition to the sober operational ways in which FRT is framed by government and state actors. Much of what we have speculated on in this chapter is driven by the critical social concerns outlined in the second half of chapter 2. This results in a set of descriptions (and attendant discussions) that might seem familiar to critics but are certainly not regularly featured in mainstream industry and policy discussions of FRT.

At this point, however, we need to refocus our attention more towards the present. As Nordmann (2007) reasons, getting too entwined with anticipating future sociotechnical forms distracts us from current concerns – especially actual risks and harms that are already arising from existing technologies. Given the thrust of the various critical issues outlined in previous chapters, engaging with the topic of the possible futures of facial recognition without giving due attention to present-day matters of injustice, inequality and resistance makes little sense. With this in mind, our concluding discussions bring us back to the present. Given everything that we now know about FRT, where should we be going next?

7

Making Critical Sense of Facial Recognition and Society

Introduction

This book has covered a lot of ground. In one sense, discussions around facial recognition are wide-ranging simply because the uses of the technology (actual and proposed) are wide ranging. The last six chapters have touched on everything from mini-webcams costing a few dollars to manufacture to multi-billion dollar assemblages of city-wide cameras, AI systems and vast photographic datasets. Yet discussions around FRT are also wide ranging and complex because facial recognition is not simply a technological matter. As we have seen, real-world uses of the technology encompass everything from the seemingly innocuous act of unlocking a smartphone through to pinpointing military attacks. At the same time, FRT is being used to find lost pets, help citizens correctly use recycling bins and prevent problem gamblers from entering casinos. It comes as no surprise, perhaps, that there is little clear agreement over the pros and cons of this technology.

Making sense of the part that FRT could play in our everyday lives (if at all) is complicated further by the rapid pace of development in computer vision, biometrics and smart-camera technology. These areas of computer science and hardware development are progressing quickly. In the time that elapses between us writing this book and you reading it, a raft of new advances, applications and potential use cases will undoubtedly emerge – bringing new sets of hopes and fears, suggesting additional possible conveniences and offering 'solutions' to problems that we previously might not have seen as problems at all.

Given all this, making sense of how facial recognition should be used in contemporary society is not something that can be quickly resolved. These are ongoing conversations that need to continue across all sectors of society – computer scientists engaging with civil society, policy makers talking with programmers, regulators speaking with system vendors – all contributing to genuine society-wide engagement with these issues. Now that the technology has been developed, interest in facial recognition is not going to fade away of its own accord. If nothing else, momentum for FRT development will continue to be driven by companies chasing profits, as well as by computer scientists eager to push the technical boundaries of what is undeniably an exacting and challenging area of technology development. Yet, while facial recognition development will undoubtedly continue for the time being, much more attention needs to be paid to the societal implications of this technological innovation and profit chasing – especially the considerable consequences for the ways in which our institutions function and how we live our lives.

The need for balanced and open discussion

In these concluding discussions, we consider what lessons might be learnt from our overview of the first 50 years or so of FRT . . . and where we might like to see this technology go next. The technology will undoubtedly continue to provoke polarized opinions and extreme views. Some readers will have come to this book with preconceived opinions that facial recognition is an inherently unwelcome and utterly dangerous development. Others will have started from an opposite viewpoint, believing facial recognition to be powerful technology that can be genuinely useful and convenient. We would hope that previous chapters have at least begun to chip away at any of these steadfast opinions. Nevertheless, it is likely that many readers arrive at the conclusion of this book with some strong opinions still intact.

In many ways, how anyone views the societal 'goods' and societal 'harms' of facial recognition depends on what version of society they experience and/or are attuned to. This is clearly not a wholly unproblematic technology. Most obviously, facial recognition clearly does discriminate against people of colour in terms of what the technology 'recognizes', and then in terms of the outcomes of these processes. It also codifies versions of gender and race, treating them as if they are objective characteristics rather than social and historical constructions. In so doing, the technology can make it harder to recognize and contest the naturalization of these categories and the forms of discrimination they have enabled. On the other hand, there are clearly other groups of people for whom facial recognition is never experienced in noticeably disadvantageous ways. As in the case of the development of technology more generally, those in positions of control find ways to turn it to their advantage so as to advance their own interests and consolidate their power. One safe prediction is that economic and political forces will shape the deployment of facial recognition to their own ends. The diverging personal experiences of technology – what Ruha Benjamin (2019) describes as 'vertical realities' of how different groups encounter the same technology – go some way to explaining why FRT is still being welcomed by many people. While many groups experience facial recognition as a technology of surveillance and control, the same technologies are experienced as sources of convenience and security by others. As Benjamin (2019: 65) reminds us, 'power is, if anything, relational. If someone is experiencing the underside of an unjust system, others, then, are experiencing its upside.'

So, in making sense of everything that has been discussed in the preceding chapters, a key starting point for our closing discussions must be one of acknowledging facial recognition as a contested technology – something that many people feel strongly opposed to, others strongly supportive of, and many more simply ambivalent or agnostic towards. In this sense, it is important to account for the rationality of *all* people and groups holding these different viewpoints. Everyone will have different assumptions and imperatives and be pursuing different (often conflicting) goals when talking about how this technology should be used. Moreover, these rationalities will surely be shaped by the social position of those who exert them. So our concluding considerations do not attempt to provide definitive judgements about the 'rights' and 'wrongs' of the development of FRT across society. Instead, we want to reflect on how things have come to be this way, and where they might be going next. This means thinking about how competing meanings of FRT have already been produced, contested and directed, *and* how we might want to influence these processes in the near future. The continued use of facial recognition in our societies is by no means a done deal. The meanings of facial recognition in society have not settled. As such, all members of society – however non-expert they might consider themselves – still have an important role to play in determining how this contentious aspect of contemporary society takes shape. So, in this spirit of reflection, what issues and arguments have emerged from the last six chapters? What have we learnt from our discussions so far?

Facial recognition: a technology that often does not work

Perhaps the most important – and certainly the most immediate – question to ask of the facial recognition applications covered in this book is 'Do they even work?' Regardless of any wider enthusiasms or concerns, when we examine the implementation of FRTs *in situ*, the most immediate challenge is often that the technology simply does not work as intended – and certainly does not work to the extent claimed by industry actors and vendors pitching to largely AI-credulous markets. This book has highlighted various instances where 'facial analysis' and 'facial detection' systems are actually capable of doing little automated detection or analysis of the sort. We have also seen incredibly fallible 'facial recognition' systems struggling to provide consistent matches with even the clearest facial images. All told, there are strong parallels with the roll-out of some facial detection systems and what Bruce Schneier (2003) has termed 'security theatre'. Just as with CCTV cameras that are never turned on, in some cases the idea that facial recognition or facial detection is present is enough for some people, regardless of whether the technology functions or not.

This question of what an emerging technology is actually capable of doing (in comparison to what its vendors claim it is capable of) is a key one that needs to be foregrounded much more prominently in critical discussions of FRT. As Meredith Broussard (2021) puts it, we need to move away from fixating on the *ex-ante* claims of the IT industry, only paying full attention to the limitations of their products much later on down the track: 'A lot of the problem we run into with AI is that people make dramatic claims about what the software can do (*ex-ante* claims) and then the analysis afterward (ex-post) reveals that the claims are false.'

We are certainly seeing this with current claims for facial detection systems that can detect emotions, or facial recognition that can pluck any individual from a crowded precinct. The best that the technology can do is generate a number of possible matches, which will be greater or smaller depending on what tolerance levels for false positives have been set in the system. Of course, there is real value in critics continuing to grapple with the potential misuses and broader logics implicit in the technological imaginaries that drive the design and development of emerging technologies. Yet critics should not be distracted by the speculative qualities attached to these technologies at the expense of engaging with their actual substance. As Deb Raji (2021) observes, 'Even AI critics will fall for the PR hype, discussing ethics in the context of some supposedly functional technology. But, often, there is no moral dilemma beyond the fact that something consequential was deployed and it doesn't work.'

Put bluntly, then, we need to pay much more attention to the consequences of the FRT that is currently being used *not* working. Equally importantly, we need to attend to the ways in which the hype underwrites future flawed uses. As past experience suggests, the fact that the technology may not live up to the hype does not prevent that very hype from being used to nonetheless justify its widespread use. It is doubtful, for example, that targeted advertising is as powerful as its proponents suggest, and yet an entire surveillance economy has grown up around it, resulting in processes of datafication and social sorting that have widespread social consequences. The fact, for example, that people have false information pumped into their news feeds is the direct result of an advertising model based on the premise that customization will boost sales. Regardless of whether sales revenues can be directly attributed to targeted ads, the entire information economy has shifted to accommodate the assumption that they work.

Already, poorly functioning FRT is leading to various significant breakdowns, disjunctures and harms that often remain unreported yet require our close attention. There is, additionally, the danger of the technology being put to use in the name of efficiency or convenience without adequate testing to see if it actually performs as advertised. Thus, as we saw in chapter 4, the inconveniences and harms associated with emerging technology like facial recognition *not* working properly clearly depend on who you are and on your life circumstances. Not being recognized by an apartment's facial recognition door-entry system is likely to have different consequences for an upper-middle-class apartment owner in Manhattan as opposed to a tenant in rent-stabilized apartments in Brooklyn (Durkin 2019). The same technological glitch takes on a very different meaning depending on the social context in which it occurs.

The difficulties of discerning 'good' uses of facial recognition

Another theme that has surfaced throughout this book is the difficulty of agreeing on what might constitute 'good' uses of any facial recognition technology. The idea that such technologies can be used for good is a popular but slippery one in current discourses around emerging technologies. This is certainly evident in growing talk around AI for Good, AI for the Common Good and ambitions for AI to be 'good for all'. For some, these 'goods' relate to global benefits – such as the development of technology to support humanitarian or environmental crisis response. For others, the idea of 'technology for good' relates to supporting increased social inclusion and economic empowerment of vulnerable populations. For some, 'good' uses of emerging technologies simply equate to the application of software and systems in public services such as health or education. Elsewhere, 'for good' uses can be those related to culture, the arts and entertainment – AI software that generates music, poetry or paintings.

All told, the idea of framing emerging technology like FRT 'for good' is beginning to attract some push-back for being deliberately nebulous and too often deployed with little genuine conviction. For example, veteran tech journalist Karen Hao (2021) suggests that tech industry talk of 'for good' should be seen simply as shorthand for 'an initiative completely tangential to your core business that helps you generate good publicity'. All too often the focus on 'good uses' backgrounds the broader question of the concentration of technological control – the issue of which companies and entities control the technology and who is subjected to it. This raises the key question of who gets to decide what constitutes a supposedly 'good' use of facial recognition. As we have seen throughout this book, one person's 'good' use of facial recognition can often prove to be another person's 'bad' use. We have also seen how even the best-case uses of facial recognition are always shadowed by potentially harmful ones. Of course, it is commendable that facial recognition developers are willing to engage in more nuanced thinking and engagement with social issues. After all, an ambition to do good brings a human focus to what might otherwise be largely technical concerns. Nevertheless, we can see how most efforts are hampered ultimately by their reliance on vague and unarticulated political assumptions about what social good might constitute (let alone the question of whether an unproblematic 'good' might be achievable at all).

At best, then, attempts so far to promote an idea of 'facial recognition for social good' have tended to fall into a non-politicized 'know it when you see it' approach to deciding what constitutes social good. This can lead quickly to ready equivalencies such as 'preventing crime = good' or 'invasion of privacy = bad'. Couching the deployment of FRT in such broad-brush terms is a convenient way of glossing over the fact that deciding what constitutes 'good' involves normative judgements which ideally should be driven by an underpinning guiding political philosophy. For example, what if the 'crime' in question is legitimate political dissent, or what if the 'privacy' in question is being used to cover up abuse? A lack of grounding principles means that the 'social goods' that facial recognition developers end up pursuing can cover a wide (and sometimes conflicting) range of political characteristics. The result is a dangerous oversimplification of issues that are politically complex and might lack clear consensus over what is desirable. In such circumstances, facial recognition developers run the risk of blithely 'wading into hotly contested political territory . . . while avoiding any actual engagement with social and political impacts' of their actions (Green 2018).

The clear-cut nature of facial recognition 'harms'

While it might be difficult to reach a consensus on 'good' uses of facial recognition, it seems far less difficult to get a clear sense of the likely harms being enacted with FRT – particularly from the groups that are experiencing these harms. Another important theme recurring throughout this book, then, is the significant capacity that facial recognition has to discriminate against and oppress already disadvantaged groups. When talking about FRT, therefore, it is important to problematize the process of being 'recognized' and to acknowledge the capacity to 'recognize' as a form of power. The previous six chapters have shown in a variety of ways that the process of 'recognizing' a person (and inferring things about them) is inherently surveillant, enacted for purposes of controlling behaviour, based around the exercise of power, and therefore oppressive. So, regardless of the conveniences of using your face to unlock a smartphone, pay for a coffee or be whisked off to a VIP lounge, we have to take seriously the ways in which FRT is used as a means of control. As Birhane and Van Dijk (2020) remind us, the most 'pressing matter' at the moment in discussions of AI, ethics and society is 'the oppressive use of AI technology against vulnerable groups in society'.

Various oppressive uses of FRT have emerged throughout this book along a number of recurring lines. Most notable are the clear problems that the technology has in terms of race – be it the technical challenges of recognizing darker skin tones through to the racialized outcomes of its implementation. Many forms of FRT can be accused of advancing what Ruha Benjamin (2019) terms 'engineered inequality'. In other words, these technologies are oppressive and disadvantaging, 'given their design in a society structured by interlocking forms of domination'. In this sense, much of what we have covered in this book lends weight to arguments from Joy Buolamwini, Safia Noble, Simone Browne, Ruha Benjamin, Timnit Gebru and many other researchers that, in view of the inherent racializing and racist logics baked into the structure of FRT, the potential harms of using these systems for even the most benign purposes in public settings render their use simply too risky. As Luke Stark puts it, this is the equivalent of using a nuclear weapon to demolish an anthill.

Also notable in previous chapters is the problematic use of FRT in terms of 'identifying' different genders and ethnicities – perpetuating harmful ideas about what it means to identify as a particular gender or ethnicity, and playing a powerful role in what Os Keyes, Hitzig and Blell (2021: 158) describe as ongoing 'scientific attempts to find, and fix, forms of identity'. In attempting to sort individuals according to demographic groupings, such approaches resuscitate and encode long-debunked categories of race into machinic forms of identification and social sorting. These particular harms highlight the inherently dehumanizing nature of FRT – a one-way, reductive, statistical gaze that seeks to view the face in terms of data points and numbers. This 'dehumanisation of the observed' (Brighenti 2010: 337) exacerbates the discriminatory effects of the technology, given the fact that those who are seen as 'less than human' historically tend to be the most marginalized people in a society – not least people of colour, ethnic minorities, women, the disabled, the elderly, the poor and various intersections thereof.

The fact that FRT leads to harm towards these particular groups is not a surprise if we consider the history of technologically facilitated surveillance back to the beginning of the twentieth century. One obvious continuity from previous surveillance technologies is the double-bind of how FRT renders minoritized groups hypervisible in many instances, while at the same time implying that minoritized people do not 'fit' within dominant data regimes (Browne 2015). Thus FRT serves to both misrecognize and oppress these groups in ways that make society-wide use of this technology profoundly inappropriate and something to be rejected and resisted. As we argued in chapter 5, developers cannot simply make FRT 'fairer' by adding more Black and brown faces into their training datasets. These groups will be minoritized, regardless of how well represented they are in the 'ground-truth' data.

It is important, therefore, to look far and wide for ways in which the harms of FRT are experienced. Most obvious is the blatant use of the technologies by oppressive regimes – not least the use of FRT by Chinese authorities in the suppression of the Uyghur population or Russian state appropriation of city-wide FRT to identify and prosecute protesters. Such examples do not solely involve FRT but, rather, show how FRT fits neatly into the logics and apparatus of state oppression. In this sense, FRT is not necessarily dehumanizing in and of itself. Rather these (mis)uses of FRT highlight the ways in which 'humans already dehumanise others through abuse and increasingly use tech to do so' (Senftt 2019).

Yet, at the same time, it remains important not to lose sight of instances of oppression and harm arising from the use of FRT that are more mundane, slight and less perceptible. As we also saw in chapter 5, this might involve the use of facial recognition check-in systems for gig workers, the insertion of facial recognition door locks by landlords looking to harass their tenants, and many other minor acts of sidelining, monitoring and control against groups that are already in vulnerable and disadvantaged situations. For those not directly experiencing facial recognition in these ways, it is perhaps possible to argue that these are simply isolated cases, and that in most instances FRT is used to little or no disadvantage. At the same time, each additional use contributes to the extension and normalization of a powerful monitoring and tracking infrastructure that concentrates control in the hands of those who operate the systems and set their priorities. In this respect, 'mundane' uses of the technology remain of a piece with the broader logics of surveillance that exacerbate power imbalances and enable oppression.

The dangers of presuming facial recognition to be neutral

We hope that this book has shown that there is plenty of room for social critics of facial recognition to develop better understandings of the technologies that they are criti- quing – especially the actual capabilities of the technology, as well as the revealed priorities for its future deployment. Wendy Chun (taking forward N. Katherine Hayles's notion of 'medium specific criticism') stresses the need for those in the social sciences and humanities to work hard to properly understand how any AI technology functions and operates before attempting to critique it (Chun 2008). This does not require everyone to become an expert in the 'esoteric' techni- calities of computer vision (in effect, bringing non-experts up to the expertise levels of a facial recognition specialist). Nevertheless, there is merit in working to increase under- standing of the broad processes of facial recognition and computer vision (see Collins and Pinch 2014).

At the same time, there is also room for those involved in the technical aspects of the FRT community to develop better awareness of the politics of their work. Recurring throughout this book have been examples of computer scientists who would prefer to see themselves as working along non-political lines – developing technology that is essentially neutral, working with data that are objective, and seeing themselves as 'just' engineers. This logic is evident in this knee-jerk reaction from a Dutch university computer scientist (in a subsequently deleted Tweet) to the use of FRT by Chinese authorities to monitor the minority Uyghur population:

The Uyghurs are facing the consequences of the use of working technology, not of a research project. . . . Most research can potentially have a wide variety of uses, both useful and harmful, and it is very tricky to predict what they are going to be. I think it's pointless to try to regulate research based on what it could potentially be used for. (Chrupała 2021)

This distinction between seeming context-free 'research', and the later 'work' that the technology is put to by others reflects Bettina Berendt's (2019) point about the dangers of seeing facial recognition in purely computational terms. Statements such as this disavowal of Chinese use of facial recognition on the Uyghur population bring us back to the key questions of what facial recognition developers see themselves as doing. Do you see the 'face' as a series of data points that can be scanned, mapped and manipulated, or do you see the 'face' as an integral and intimate part of a person's identity? Is the face a three-dimensional object that can be scoped, scanned and captured? Are you solving a complex computational problem of matching data points with other sets of aggregated data points, or are you personally identifying a living social human being – a person with all the connotations and connections implicit in living in a society that already thinks that it 'knows' you in a variety of different ways? When described and justified along these divergent lines, it is perhaps not surprising that the development and deployment of FRT continue to be contentious issues.

This distancing of FRT development from its application can be seen as a major problem. Indeed, some critics equate researchers working on FRT development with scientists refining plutonium on the 1940s Manhattan Project – a breakthrough that enabled the rapid deployment of the Hiroshima and Nagasaki nuclear bombs (Stark 2019). Computer vision and FRT scientists should, according to this comparison, similarly recognize themselves as political actors, and ground their actions accordingly. Just as some of the Manhattan Project scientists issued grave warnings, so too should facial recognition developers and researchers. There are certainly compelling arguments for the claim that, as a technology, in the abstract, facial recognition is in its very nature antithetical to democratic commitments and human rights. Along the same lines as the comparison to plutonium, Hartzog and Selinger (2015) argue that 'the mere existence of facial recognition systems, which are often invisible, harms civil liberties'. The deeper point they are making is that there is no such thing as an abstract deployment of technology – such systems are always embedded in the social relations that shape their use and are in turn influenced by their exercise.

With this fact in mind, critical scholars contend that any computer scientist presenting themselves (or their actions) as apolitical is taking a political stance. Harvard applied mathematician Ben Green argues that any computer scientist attempting to claim neutrality is taking a 'fundamentally conservative' position that signals implicit support for maintaining the status quo and, therefore, the interests of dominant social groups and hegemonic political values. As such, it makes no sense for anyone working within computer vision or facial recognition to claim neutrality, or to consider themselves to be somehow operating 'outside of politics'. No computer science can be carried out in the expectation of simply discovering 'knowledge for knowledge's sake'. Despite the claims of some in the computer vision and facial recognition communities, there is no detached 'scientific rationality' that sits above societal concerns. Nor is there any technology that can be fully dissociated from the character of the society in which it is embedded.

This means that is it important to see the deployment of FRT across society in appropriately nuanced terms. As many of the examples highlighted in this book suggest, in societies based on hyper-commercialization, facial recognition will be used to enhance and accelerate the forms of behaviour that foster consumption. Similarly, facial recognition will enable more efficient and oppressive forms of discrimination in racist societies and forward the interests of dominant groups in societies that are socially stratified. At the same time, however, no society is monolithic and no ruling group all powerful – there will always be social divisions and cultural contradictions that provide openings for challenging existing social relations. Therefore, we are likely to encounter deployments of the technology that run counter to the imperatives of existing authorities – such as the use of facial recognition technology by street protesters to identify police officers who deliberately cover their badges to thwart public accountability. At times, social and technological forces align to dramatically transform social relations, but there is no guarantee this will happen, nor is there any guarantee that the result will be an improvement on what came before. The dominant tendency will be for existing social dynamics to be reinforced and exacerbated by the deployment of any new technologies.

Acknowledging the oppressive potential of facial recognition along these lines does not extend to blaming individual computer vision researchers for the consequences of their design and development work. Yet it is important for those experts working in the fields of computer vision, biometrics and FRT development to assume some degree of collective responsibility, especially for how facial recognition developers, designers and vendors choose to engage with the harms arising from the use of the technologies they produce. As Ruha Benjamin (2019: 62) observes, harmful consequences of FRT might not be the 'fault' of individual programmers but are certainly the fault of 'the norms and structures of the tech industry' and the societal contexts in which the tech industry operates.

Looking towards a society shaped by facial recognition

At this point, then, we can take stock of everything discussed in this chapter and relate it to the social theory concerns that were introduced in chapter 2 and subsequently expanded on in later chapters. Regardless of the points just outlined, what implications does the continued implementation of FRTs have for the societies that we live in? What might we expect from a life that is increasingly underpinned by facial recognition?

A society where 'your face is your ID'

Facial recognition clearly marks a continuation of surveillance logics that have long been in place through the societal infusion of closed-circuit TV cameras and other forms of visual surveillance technology. Such systems have already shaped our expectation that when, for example, a crime takes place or an exceptional event occurs, it can be reconstructed through recourse to the images captured and stored on ubiquitous surveillance cameras. These systems have fuelled the 'recognitive imaginary' by flooding us with images in need of further information. As such, facial recognition comes to fill a gap that seems increasingly obvious. Police may no longer have to issue pleas for assistance in helping to recognize 'persons of interest' captured on cameras. Instead, FRTs and facial analytics can organize, categorize and make sense of the flood of visual information being collected. First there is the (attempted) recognition of faces and objects, then patterns, behaviours, sentiments and, finally, intentions. All of this will be understood through the unique identifying label of one's face. Referring back to the idea of the 'face as meta-data' outlined in chapter 6, the facial recognition society is based around individuals being tagged at all times with contextual information in the form of their faces – information that can be read passively, at a distance, to identify them throughout the course of the day.

A society predicated around concerns of security and control

We have considered a range of possible uses for FRT throughout this book, covering everything from reuniting families separated by natural disasters to recognizing VIPs in casinos. On balance, however, security and control emerge as the driving impulses behind the development and deployment of the technology. Other uses may well get grafted onto this impulse (such as being able to target advertising displays more effectively), but these serve as ancillary drivers, dual-use cases and sometimes even alibis for the widespread deployment of facial recognition. Of course, some uses (such as matching individuals with their identity for access to public transport or an ATM) remain relatively delimited in as much as they take place only in certain places or at particular times. However, the imperative of security and control pushes in the direction of the ubiquitous deployment of the technology – the ability to recognize everyone, wherever they go, for whatever purpose.

The unrealistic desire for total visuality

Following on from this latter point is a deeper imperative that marks a convergence between commerce and security – the ambition to collect as much information as possible to manage risk and maximize opportunity. This might be seen as a defining attribute of modernity's link between knowledge and control. As Isabel Capeloa Gil (2020: 94) puts it, 'the organization around plans of total visuality . . . encompass simultaneously utter control and utter sight'. Total visuality marks what might be described as the disloc- ation and distribution of 'seeing' from the realm of the human viewing subject to that of the 'smart' environment that is saturated with sensors. Nevertheless, even if it were possible to equip all of the billion existing surveillance cameras with facial recognition technology, the prospect of 'utter vision' remains a long way off (Cosgrove 2019). The existing camera networks are, in many cases, operated by a patchwork of local governments, federal agencies, private institutions and commercial entities. Getting all these systems to connect to one another would be a monumental task, even in a highly centralized authoritarian regime, let alone countries that consider themselves based on a democratic system of governance and its associated civil rights, including freedom of assembly and speech.

The likely limited forms of 'low-stakes' facial recognition deployment by institutions

Given the cost and technical challenges of creating such an all-seeing system, it is likely that, for the foreseeable future, facial recognition technology will be mainly deployed in relatively delimited, low-stakes contexts (with the exception of law enforcement, intelligence and military uses). These will be use cases where alternative backup systems will remain available in the case of the FRT failing, or else in contexts where people are willing to tolerate a relatively high degree of error. For example, in the near future, we are most likely to find the development of the infrastructure for facial recognition systems following the contours of a logic of convenience and cost. We are already seeing relatively widespread uptake in contexts where the technology is quite accurate (as in the case of one-to-one face matching) and/or the cost of error is relatively low (such as having to find another form of payment for your coffee). Nevertheless, questions need to be asked of those who are able to make this decision to continue using what is clearly an imperfect technology – in other words, for whom are the stakes perceived as 'low'? The cost of errors in the system, which can be difficult to prove because of the proprietary character of the algorithms, falls disproportionately on misidentified criminal suspects, rejected job applicants, and others in similar vulnerable position of needing to be correctly 'recognized' and 'known'.

The normalization of facial recognition through personal 'convenience' and 'suspicionless surveillance'

The acceptance and adoption of this technology by individuals is likely to be driven by perceptions of personal convenience combined with the imperative of security. Of course, the promise of increased convenience is addressed to a particular demographic – those most likely to be at the receiving end of the benefits of the targeted social sorting enabled by facial recognition technology. Those who will be most advantaged will be already privileged groups such as world travellers, affluent credit card users, and those who do not encounter forms of discrimination or persecution because of their identities. At the other end of the spectrum are people whose identities might be used against them. This does not just include those engaged in a range of criminal behaviour but also undocumented migrants and asylum seekers and, depending on the jurisdiction, political protesters, ethnic minorities, dissidents and members of the LGBTQIA+ community. History indicates that the socially and economically disadvantaged are also likely targets of oppressive uses of automated technology.

The boundary between advantaged and disadvantaged groups may be less clear than it seems at first glance. Facial recognition technology, because of its passive, embedded, and potentially ubiquitous nature, enables what Knutson (2021) describes as 'suspicionless surveillance' – an ongoing 'fishing expedition' for all kinds of information about individuals for a potentially undelimited set of purposes. The result is a threat not only to civil rights and the freedoms we associate with democratic self-governance but also to the social fabric. A society cannot function without an underlying layer of social trust, but 'suspicionless surveillance' is the flip side of a generalized and corrosive suspicion. In short, in a context where surveillance becomes universalized, then, in principle, anyone is a potential suspect. This therefore raises concerns over the changing nature of sociality and social trust in light of the increased deployment of FRT. In short, facial recognition will frame everyone who passes in front of the cameras as a potential suspect. This raises a likely fundamental degradation of society – it is impossible to construct a viable version of sociality on the principle of universal suspicion, just as it is impossible to develop systems of surveillance comprehensive enough to replace social trust.

Reduced democratic freedoms

This latter point raises the potential threat to democracy posed by the widespread deployment of facial recognition. As a political system, democracy must necessarily provide the space for dissent and disagreement, as well as a certain amount of personal freedom and control over what one reveals about oneself to others. The same is true of social life more generally. As Slavoj Žižek (2020) has noted, the basis of our coexistence is some minimum level of idealization with respect to one another. Social life entails a degree of abstraction away from all the details of one another's behaviours, desires and innermost thoughts. As social beings, we rely on the freedom to not *always* divulge what we are really thinking or how we really feel. Indeed, the functioning of social life at all levels depends on this freedom and on the forms of judgement and discretion it involves. A world in which we could all read each other's thoughts on the surfaces of our faces would be a nightmare, and would likely divest us of our ability to trust or believe in one another.

As we have seen in various examples throughout this book, facial recognition threatens to alter this balance. The social threat posed by FRT, then, is to facilitate the matching of data about an identified individual across a range of databases (by using the face as a universal identifier) and by its ability to fold a growing range of activities and behaviour into this database. In particular is the curtailing of the autonomy that lies at the heart of how we have come to understand what it means to be human subjects and citizens. It is this sense of relative autonomy – without which democratic self-governance becomes impossible – that is enshrined in what might be described as our fundamental 'digital rights'. As Kelly Gates (2011: 194) puts it in her seminal account of facial recognition technology, 'Whether intentionally or not, applying a standardized way of seeing the face to others can deny those embodied subjects their independent existence, their own ability to speak for, represent, and exist for themselves.' The threat of total surveillance, we have suggested, might not be immediate (or indeed possible), yet it remains as an endpoint towards which the logics of facial recognition and other forms of data-driven surveillance are directed. This fact is, in itself, cause for serious concern and for the need to respond to the future trajectory of facial recognition technology in the present.

Conclusions

Making sense of the role that facial recognition is set to play in our societies – and the responses that this might merit – is a difficult balancing act. In this chapter, we have highlighted some crucial lines of distinction that need to be kept in mind when deciding what forms of FRT might be deemed acceptable (if not desirable) in our everyday lives. This is technology that is *not* capable of fully living up to its claimed capabilities, but it is likely to be deployed nonetheless. It is technology that offers considerable levels of personal convenience and security but also carries a considerable threat to our civil rights and democratic freedoms, while also exacerbating existing social divisions and disadvantage.

It is therefore possible to imagine the best – and worst – of all worlds arising from the continued take-up of FRTs across society. On one hand, we can envision the prospect of seamless mobility across social settings – rarely having to stop to prove who we are or what we want to do. Moreover, we can be assured that those around us are well intentioned and unthreatening. All told, we can feel reassured in our recognition. Conversely, as we speculated towards the end of chapter 6, the ultimate 'integral accident' (in Paul Virilio's words) associated with FRT is a recurring loop of automated misidentification and the accident of total misrecognition.

One can imagine the absurd resulting deadlock – the people around you may know who you are, but their knowledge is helpless in the face of the malfunctioning machine. Such is the dystopian vision prepared for us by the offloading of sociality onto automated systems and the replacement of face-to-face interaction by the interface of FRT.

Therefore, the critical question that now needs to be addressed is where we want to go from here. As we posited at the beginning of this book, the future of facial recognition depends on how we choose to use it, and who the 'we' end up being. There is no inevitable 'technological future' for facial recognition – except, as Kelly Gates (2011: 198) has pointed out, in the marketing hype: 'the idea that the widespread deployment of these technologies is an inevitable part of a non-negotiable future plays an important role in their implementation, but the automation of face perception has never been a foregone conclusion.' With this thought in mind, the final brief epilogue offers a number of different ways in which 'we' might choose to progress from here.

Epilogue: Facial Recognition – So Where Now?

Introduction

Despite the concerns raised throughout this book (especially in the previous chapter), critics of facial recognition are fighting an uphill battle. Even in the face of the high-profile protests against police (mis)use of FRT, the advent of municipal bans and so on, the past few years have seen the steady (and often unremarked) advancement of the technology into many aspects of everyday life. As we have detailed, these applications are often tucked away in the background of our daily digital practices, in our smart-phones, social media and laptops. The process of being 'facially recognized' is integrated into activities that most people rarely give much thought to anyway – paying for a coffee, walking past an advertising billboard. Some of these applications of facial recognition are in places where people are already resigned to giving up some of their usual expectations of privacy and surveillance, such as casinos, football stadiums and during online examinations. However controversial facial recognition might be considered by some, this technology is becoming normalized in front of our eyes.

Regardless of any criticisms and concerns, take-up of FRT will undoubtedly continue to grow throughout the 2020s and beyond. Whether or not these facial technologies 'work' as promised by developers and vendors, this technology looks set to be steadily integrated into our societies and social settings. As Adam Greenfield (2018: 243) puts it, 'the meaningful question isn't whether these technologies work as advertised. It's whether someone believes that they do, and acts on that belief.'

Against this background, we need to treat the continued societal integration of FRTs as a serious proposition with specific politics. As stressed in the previous chapter, it is important to ask questions about the distinct social order that is being built up around facial recognition – i.e. likely reconfigurations of power, (dis)advantage, social knowledge and social relations within public and private spaces, in our workplaces, in our neighbourhoods and homes. When approached in these terms, there is much about the continued deployment of FRT that merits our active attention. As reiterated throughout this book, no technology is inevitable – all technologies are shaped to some extent by the societies in which they are produced and used. How FRT unfolds over the next couple of decades remains an open question. We have reached a moment where there are a number of different ways that we might collectively choose to proceed. In this concluding epilogue, we briefly consider three possible ways in which facial recognition might continue to unfold.

The path of least resistance

The first option is to conclude that there is ultimately not much to be concerned about. From this perspective, FRT does not warrant any particular censure or concern. While most applications of FRT might not work perfectly all the time, one could reason that we ought to consider whether we are satisfied with the pre-existing alternative ways of doing things. Inconsistencies, faulty decision making, social bias and systematic discrimination long pre-date the development of facial recognition technology. Indeed, it could be argued that the increased use of facial recognition systems, at least in some contexts, has offered a measure of redress to systemic bias in policing, housing, employment and credit. We might also take some reassurance in the observation that the hype far outstrips the actual deployment of facial recognition. In this sense, we perhaps need not get overly concerned by capabilities that still remain largely speculative. Like augmented reality and self-driving cars, the most dystopian forms of FRT seem far from being developed (even if they are technically possible at all). As such, this might be something we need not devote too much time to in the wake of other more pressing concerns. Moreover, those with faith in the power of the market might also be reassured that any applications that are seen as too controversial will eventually prove to not be profitable enough to develop and implement.

As such, developers of facial recognition technology might well feel that this technology has been unduly demonized in recent years, while many *other* forms of detailed information capture have been allowed to multiply online with minimal regulation. In this sense, it could be argued that facial recognition has been caught squarely within the recent backlash against surveillance capitalism. A brief scan of the editorial headlines suggests that, at least for the moment, there is a strong push towards regulating the technology before it is too late. The *Guardian* (2019) has called the technology 'a danger to democracy'; the journal *Nature* (2020) has called for an 'ethical reckoning' with facial recognition technology; and *Scientific American* has argued in favour of more regulation. There is certainly a political skew in this response, perhaps in part because much of the concern about bias and accuracy has come mainly from those with a progressive sensibility. In contrast, the conservative *National Review* in the United States contends that FRT will bring us 'closer to utopia than dystopia' (2019).

Another possible reason for going along with the continued deployment of FRT is that many different forms of it have already been implemented surreptitiously. In short, attempts to restrict this technology might well be too little, too late. Stadia, casinos and other private venues are already equipping their surveillance camera systems with facial recognition, often without public notification or consent. Recent public backlash and negative reporting against the technology has led those who deploy facial recognition to find ways of surreptitiously putting their systems to use while evading public and media attention. In the absence of concerted, comprehensive forms of regulation, it is likely that a range of uses of the technology will be implemented for both security and commercial purposes. It is possible that some of these uses will turn out to be practical and economic failures while others may provide the symbolic comfort of what we referred to in chapter 7 as 'security theatre'. Still others may deliver on their promises. Even if these successful applications of FRT result in the consolidation of power in the hands of those who can afford to own and operate the technology, this is not a criticism unique to facial recognition. For all these reasons, then, there might be simply little point in putting up too much opposition to what already appears to be a technological reality of contemporary society.

Complete prohibition

On the other hand, there is the opposite argument for enacting a complete ban on all forms of FRT, both currently existing and emergent. Here it could be argued that facial recognition is one of an array of emerging technologies – including, for example, lethal autonomous weapons and cloning – that merit an outright ban. According to Woodrow Hartzog and Evan Selinger (2015), professors in law and philosophy respectively, 'the future of human flourishing depends on facial recognition technology being banned before the systems become too entrenched in our lives.' Hartzog and Selinger's stance is that even seemingly innocuous or beneficial uses of the technology serve as an alibi for a technology that is 'intrinsically oppressive' because the harm-to-benefit ratio is so tilted towards unaccountable forms of control. It is perhaps testimony to the rhetoric of digital futurism that at first glance this argument seems fantastical – surely it is futile to attempt to completely ban this (or any other) technology?

Yet, as Simone Browne (2021) notes, these questions have been part of FRT development since its inception, with Woody Bledsoe himself raising the basic question, 'Should I continue?'. More than 50 years later, growing numbers of critics contend that the same question needs to be asked urgently by those following in Bledsoe's path. Indeed, some critics contend that this is technology that should be rolled back altogether, akin to the outlawing of dangerous chemicals and elements. As Chris Gilliard (2021) reasons: 'One of the arguments people like to make is that you can't go back on particular technologies . . . That's patently untrue. No one would look at asbestos and say, "Well, you can't outlaw chemistry." But they look at facial recognition and say, "You can't outlaw math."'

Those arguing for outright prohibition of FRT recognize the challenges that their stance is likely to incur. Indeed, the rise of digital technology as an important adjunct to (and extension of) finance capital mitigates against a total ban. Nations have tended to be reluctant to cross swords with Big Tech and the GAFAM corporations, given their role over the past 20 years or so as an engine of financial speculation and the concentration of economic and informational power. Large fortunes are at stake as well as national reputations and military advantage. While it would certainly be feasible to ban FRT for a range of very specific purposes (as has already happened in some US jurisdictions), an outright ban seems unlikely. There is, as Hartzog and Selinger (2015) suggest, too strong a convergence of state and commercial interests in the forms of surveillance enabled by automated facial recognition, and too little organized public resistance (perhaps compounded by too much fascination with the futuristic novelty of the technology).

Those involved in developing FRT will also remind us – in highly speculative terms – of the cost of any ban. They will ask us whether we are really prepared to give up on the prospect of a technology that could make unsolved crimes a thing of the past, knowing that by the time it is possible to prove them wrong, the technology will already be in widespread use. They will remind us of the large amounts of money lost to fraud and identity theft and reiterate the digital-era promise that the enhanced ability to monitor, track and record can help minimize risk and maximize efficiency. Under these circumstances, a widespread ban of FRT would certainly require a level of public education and organization that seems highly unlikely under current conditions. In our option, we should not discount this stance altogether, yet we should remain realistic about what is being demanded here.

Strong and open scrutiny

Finally, then, is a third option of continuing to subject this technology to sustained strong scrutiny. The fact that FRT has already received significant critical attention by activists, pundits and regulators suggests that it is unlikely to get the relatively free pass previously enjoyed by other digital monitoring technologies early on in their development. We are, perhaps, starting to learn something from our mistakes. At the same time, a range of applications of the technology is being rolled out along different fronts in the attempt to normalize its use. What we described in chapter 7 as 'low-stakes' uses (such as unlocking one's smartphone) help accustom people to facial recognition by making it part of the rhythm of everyday life. At the same time, police and security applications are being rolled out in many jurisdictions without public notification or scrutiny. If these applications work their way into the regular retinue of tools used by law enforcement officers, it may be difficult to roll back the use of the technology without triggering complaints that police are being deprived of a useful investigative tool.

To limit the potential harmful effects of the technology, it is therefore important to foster robust public discussion and to ensure transparency regarding how and where it is being deployed. That the industry and those who implement its products have little incentive to draw attention to its deployment suggests an implicit recognition of the potential risks to democracy and civil rights. Thus any discussion will have to be driven by the public sector and public interest groups, including political representatives, regulators, educators and civil society groups. Our hope is that books such as this one might help indicate some future directions for public discussion and public education about facial recognition technology. As Frank Pasquale (2020: 127) reasons, this could lead to a consensus that, for example, state use of the technology as a means of addressing significant societal issues, such as terrorism or global pandemics, might be justified whereas 'to deploy such powerful technology to ticket speeders, ferret out benefit fraud, or catch petty thieves is like using a sledgehammer to kill a fly.'

It will be important for the public to have a basic understanding of its capabilities and limitations. As we saw in chapter 1, facial recognition has been repeating through the 'hype cycle' since the 2000s, but it looks positioned to become a more prevalent part of the 2020s technological landscape. There is a self-stoking dynamic that characterizes the deployment of the technology: the more widely it is used, the more data will be generated for training purposes, the more accurate the systems will become, and the greater the justification for its more widespread use. As the technology becomes more prevalent, controlling its use will become an increasingly important social issue.

Concluding thoughts

Where we choose to go from here needs to be the subject of rigorous and sustained dialogue and discussion. As social scientists, our own sensibilities lean towards cautionary interventionist approaches rather than more laissez-faire options. We would argue that 'the path of least resistance' – that which leaves the deployment of the technology to the machinations of the market – is likely to result in the unaccountable concentration of power in the hands of public and private authorities. This level of asymmetric control over information is antithetical to democratic forms of governance and threatens fundamental human and civil rights. The outcome will be different for different countries, based on whether the technology is more or less centralized and more or less concentrated in private versus public institutions, but in all cases it is likely to pose a threat to civil rights and democratic commitments.

Nevertheless, this is a debate that needs more than just our voices and opinions. While there are clear reasons for those involved in the development of FRT to be enthused and excited by their work, this does not grant a free pass. We would argue, for example, that the technology should be prevented from claims to identify race and gender, and other inferential uses should be subject to inspection and regulation to prevent discrimination and false claims of accuracy. The use of facial recognition by law enforcement should be subject to a system of judicial warrants similar to that used for wiretapping and other forms of law enforcement surveillance. To achieve any of this, it will be crucial to ensure that the public becomes 'biometric literate' via education programmes that highlight the capabilities and limitations of the technology – in particular to dispel the notion that computers can recognize people in the ways that humans do (rather than simply assessing the likelihood of a match). It will also be important to train a generation of developers, designers and computer scientists in the social issues raised by the use of the technology and to instil in them a commitment to civic values and civil rights. This technology must only be used in ways that are publicly transparent and accountable, and subject to impact assessment where the use is seen to be socially desirable.

Moreover, there is no commandment from on high that emerging technologies *cannot* be regulated. We would argue for the need to develop legislation that keeps pace with advances in the technology and to ensure that it is enforced. There are, in many cases, already existing privacy protections that are not enforced in practice, largely because, without public awareness and concern, the political will is lacking. It will be important to provide public regulators and civil society organizations with access to information about the use of the technology that will enable them to target bad-faith deployment of facial recognition. We should remain very wary about the commercialization of the technology and ensure that democracy and civil rights trump the profit imperative. This is a technology with profound consequences for free speech, autonomy and democracy, and these should not be compromised in the pursuit of profit.

Additionally, the algorithms upon which facial recognition systems rely should be made available for testing for bias and accuracy on a regular basis to independent regulatory authorities beyond existing arbiters such as NIST. Requiring public validation might help put the brakes on the deployment of the technology, especially if robust public awareness efforts provide people with more information about the potential benefits and risks of the technology. Above all, we need to prevent the development of facial recognition systems that adopt the established business model of the internet predicated on the wholesale, speculative collection of huge data troves on the assumption that the data might be useful down the road for a range of as yet unspecified purposes.

These arguments notwithstanding, recent history does not make us particularly optimistic about FRT receiving the level of regulation, oversight, public scrutiny and delib-eration it deserves. As far as many institutional authorities are concerned, FRT undoubtedly looks like too powerful a 'fix' to merit jeopardizing during a time when automation promises to improve efficiency and effectiveness at every turn. Yet this book has highlighted a number of potential threats to democracy, freedom of expression and personal autonomy posed by the widespread implementation of the technology. Moreover, it is just as important to consider the potential of less tangible social losses – not least that any development of machines that 'recognize' us hollows out the very notion of recognition. Drawing on the work of Levinas, Grant Bollmer (2017: 69) argues that, 'Facial expression provides knowledge that subjectivity is relational, overflowing, and collective. Seeing the face of another and recognizing that face as the face of another is a foundational act that defines one both as an individual and as an essentially social being.'

This is an apt set of points on which to conclude. While this technology is widely touted as capable of 'recognition', if we accept that it is precisely this foundational act that is unavailable to the machine, then there is sufficient reason to think more carefully about the extent to which we are willing to rely upon its gaze.

References

Achiume, T. (2020). *Report of the Special Rapporteur on Contemporary Forms of Racism, Racial Discrimination, Xenophobia and Related Intolerance*. UNHCR, 10 November. https://www.ohchr.org/EN/newyork/Documents/A-75-590-AUV.docx

ACM (2020). Statement on Principles and Prerequisites for the Development, Evaluation and Use of Unbiased Facial Recognition Technologies. *ACM US Technology Policy Committee*, 30 June. https://www.acm.org/binaries/content/assets/public-policy/ustpc-facial-recognition-tech-statement.pdf

Adelaide Advertiser (2019). Skycity Adelaide Installs Facial Recognition to Catch Barred Gamblers. *Adelaide Advertiser*, 29 November. https://www.adelaidenow.com.au/business/sa-business-journal/skycity-adelaide-installs-facial-recognition-to-catch-barred-gamblers/news-story/92eb61228b0b8bcbfecc69283050f02b

Alang, N. (2018). Beware the New Military–Technology Complex. *The Week*, 24 May. www.theweek.com/articles/774633/beware-new-militarytechnology-complex

Allbright, A. (2019). If You Give a Judge a Risk Score. www. law.harvard.edu/programs/olin_center/Prizes/2019-1.pdf

Amazon (2020). https://www.aboutamazon.com/news/policy-news-views/we-are-implementing-a-one-year-moratorium-on-police-use-of-rekognition

Andrejevic, M. (2020). *Automated Media*. Routledge.

Atanasoski, N. and Vora, K. (2019). *Surrogate Humanity: Race, Robots, and the Politics of Technological Futures*. Duke University Press.

Baraniuk, C. (2020). Why COVID may mean more facial recognition tech. *BBC News*, 4 December. https://www.bbc.com/news/business-54959193

Bass, D. and Bergen, M. (2021). Facial Recognition Marches Forward, No Matter What Facebook Says. *Bloomberg*, 11 November. https://news.bloomberglaw.com/private-equity/facial-recognition-marches-forward-no-matter-what-facebook-says

Bauman, Z. and Lyon, D. (2013). *Liquid Surveillance*. Polity Press.

Benjamin, R. (2019). *Race after Technology*. Polity Press.

Berendt, B. (2019). AI for the Common Good? *Paladyn, Journal of Behavioural Robotics* 10(1): 44–65.

Birhane, A. and Van Dijk, J. (2020, February). Robot Rights? *Proceedings of the AAAI/ACM Conference on AI, Ethics, and Society*, pp. 207–13.

Bollmer, G. (2017). Empathy Machines. *Media International Australia* 165(1): 63–76.

Borak, M. (2020). iQiyi, China's Netflix, has Facial Recognition for Animated Characters. *South China Morning Post*, 13 July. www.scmp.com/abacus/tech/article/3092680/iqiyi-chinas-netflix-has-facial-recognition-animated-characters

Boyd, A. (2020). Intel Agencies Seek to Perfect Biometric Recognition from Drones, 11 December. *Nextgov*. www.nextgov.com/emerging-tech/2020/12/intel-agencies-seek-perfect-biometric-recognition-drones/170712/

Brandom, R. (2020). Moscow's Facial Recognition System

Can Be Hijacked for Just $200, Report Shows. *The Verge*, 11 November

Brighenti, A. (2010). *Visibility in Social Theory and Social Research*. Palgrave Macmillan.

Broussard, M. (2021). Tweet. 22 April, https://twitter.com/merbroussard/status/13849340025791488800

Browne, S. (2015). *Dark Matters*. Duke University Press.

Browne, S. (2021). Presentation to Microsoft '*Race & Technology*' Seminar Series, 27 October. https://www.microsoft.com/en-us/research/event/race-technology-a-research-lecture-series/#!videos

Buolamwini, J. and Gebru, T. (2018). Gender Shades: Intersectional Accuracy Disparities in Commercial Gender Classification. *Conference on Fairness, Accountability and Transparency*. PMLR, pp. 77–91.

Burgess, M. (2021). Europe Makes the Case to Ban Biometric Surveillance. *Wired*, 7 July. https://www.wired.co.uk/article/europe-ai-biometrics

Burt, C. (2020). Face Biometrics Forecast to Surpass $15B by 2027 as Verticals and Applications Expand. *Biometric Update*, 20 July. https://www.biometricupdate.com/202007/face-biometrics-forecast-to-surpass-15b-by-2027-as-verticals-and-applications-expand

Carlo, S. (2019). (Cited) Prison Facial Recognition Technology Could Deter Smuggling. *Tech Monitor*, 6 March. https://techmonitor.ai/techonology/data/prison-facial-recognition-technology

Celis, C. (2020). Critical Surveillance Art in the Age of Machine Vision and Algorithmic Governmentality. *Surveillance & Society* 18(3): 295–311.

de Certeau, M. (1984). *The Practice of Everyday Life*. University of California Press.

Chen, S. (2017). Should We Teach Facial Recognition Technology about Race? *Wired*, 15 November.

Chen, S. (2019). No Escape? Chinese VIP Jail Puts AI monitors in Every Cell 'to Make Prison Breaks Impossible'. 1 April, *South China Morning Post*. www.scmp.com/news/china/

science/article/3003903/no-escape-chinese-vip-jail-puts-ai-monitors-every-cell-make

Chiu, K. (2020). Alipay Allows Pet Owners to Buy Insurance by Using Facial Recognition on Their Cats and Dogs. *South China Morning Post*, 21 June. https://www.scmp.com/abacus/tech/article/3094053/alipay-allows-pet-owners-buy-insurance-using-facial-recognition-their

Chrupała, G. (2021). 9 June. Referenced in part in https://twitter.com/rajiinio/status/1402609650843803650

Chun, W. (2008). *Power and Paranoia in the Age of Fibre.* MIT Press.

Cole, S. (2009). *Suspect Identities: A History of Fingerprinting and Criminal Identification.* Harvard University Press.

Collins, H. and Pinch, T. (2014). *The Golem*, 2nd edn. University of Cambridge Press

Conger, K., Fausset, R. and Kovaleski, S. (2019). San Francisco Bans Facial Recognition Technology. *New York Times*, 14 May. https://www.nytimes.com/2019/05/14/us/facial-recognition-ban-san-francisco.html

Cosgrove, E. (2019). One Billion Surveillance Cameras Will be Watching around the World in 2021, a New Study Says. *CNBC*, 6 December. www.cnbc.com/2019/12/06/one-billion-surveillance-cameras-will-be-watching-globally-in-2021.html

Costandza-Chock, S. (2021). Tweet. 5 January. https://twitter.com/schock/status/1346478831255789569

Crawford, K. (2017). 20 Lessons on Bias in Machine Learning Systems. https://hub.packtpub.com/20-lessons-bias-machine-learning-systems-nips-2017/

Curran, D. and Smart, A. (2021). Data-Driven Governance, Smart Urbanism and Risk-Class Inequalities. *Urban Studies* 58(3): 487–506.

Daub, A. (2020). *What Tech Calls Thinking.* Macmillan.

Deleuze, G. (2007). *Two Regimes of Madness, Texts and Interviews, 1975–1995*, ed. D. Lapoujade. MIT Press.

Dewan, M., Murshed, M. and Lin, F. (2019). Engagement

Detection in Online Learning. *Smart Learning Environments* 6(1): 1–20.

Dixit, P. (2019). India is Creating a National Facial Recognition System, and Critics are Afraid of What Will Happen Next. *Buzzfeed*, 9 October. https://www.buzzfeednews.com/article/pranavdixit/india-is-creating-a-national-facial-recognition-system-and

Dragiewicz, M., Burgess, J., Matamoros-Fernández, A. et al. (2018). Technology Facilitated Coercive Control. *Feminist Media Studies* 18(4): 609–25.

Durkin, E. (2019). New York Tenants Fight as Landlords Embrace Facial Recognition Cameras. *Guardian*, 30 May. https://www.theguardian.com/cities/2019/may/29/new-york-facial-recognition-cameras-apartment-complex

Economist (2018). Does China's Digital Police State have Echoes in the West? *The Economist*, 2 June. www.economist.com/leaders/2018/05/31/does-chinas-digital-police-state-have-echoes-in-the-west

Edwards, P. (1996). *The Closed World*. MIT Press.

Ekman, P. (1973). *Darwin and Facial Expression: A Century of Research in Review*. Academic Press.

European Parliament (2021). Regulation on a European Approach for Artificial Intelligence, 14 April. https://www.politico.eu/wp-content/uploads/2021/04/14/AI-Draft.pdf

FaceFirst (2017). *The Five Minute Guide to Face Recognition for Event Security*. www.facefirst.com/wp-content/uploads/2017/05/The_Five_Minute_Guide_to_Face_Recognition_for_Event_Security.pdf

Feathers, T. (2021). Facial Recognition Failures are Locking People Out of Unemployment Systems. *Vice*, 19 June. https://www.vice.com/en/article/5dbywn/facial-recognition-failures-are-locking-people-out-of-unemployment-systems

Feldman Barrett, L. (2021). Tweet: Detecting Facial Movements Does Not Equal Detecting Emotion. https://twitter.com/LFeldmanBarrett/status/1408535178599878663

Foucault, M. (2007 [1975]). *Discipline and Punish*. Duke University Press.

Fox, J. (2018). What Do Cameras Do? *World Records* 1(1): 1–7. https://vols.worldrecordsjournal.org/01/01

Fussell, S. (2019). How an Attempt at Correcting Bias in Tech Goes Wrong. *The Atlantic*, 9 October. www.theatlantic.com/technology/archive/2019/10/google-allegedly-used-homeless-train-pixel-phone/599668/

Fussell, S. (2021). The Next Target for a Facial Recognition Ban? *Wired*, 28 January. https://www.wired.com/story/next-target-facial-recognition-ban-new-york/

Gates, K. (2011). *Our Biometric Future: Facial Recognition Technology and the Culture of Surveillance*. New York University Press

Gershgorn, D. (2019). This is How the US Military's Massive Facial Recognition System Works. *One Zero*, 7 November. https://onezero.medium.com/exclusive-this-is-how-the-u-s-militarys-massive-facial-recognition-system-works-bb764291b96d

Gil, I. C. (2020). 'The Global Eye or Foucault Rewired', in D. Bachmann-Medick, J. Kugele and A. Nunning (eds), *Futures of the Study of Culture*. De Gruyter.

Gilliard, C. (2018). Friction-free Racism. *Real Life*, 15 October. https://reallifemag.com/friction-free-racism/

Gilliard, C. (2020). Caught in the Spotlight. *Urban Omnibus*, 9 January. https://urbanomnibus.net/2020/01/caught-in-the-spotlight/

Gilliard, C. (2021). Chris Gilliard Sees Digital Relining in Surveillance Tech. *Washington Post*, 17 September. www.washingtonpost.com/technology/2021/09/16/chris-gilliard-sees-digital-redlining-in-surveillance-tech/

Gilmore, G. (2017). *Facial Recognition AI Will Use Your Facial Expressions to Judge Creditworthiness*, 30 October. https://glengilmore.medium.com/facial-recognition-ai-will-use-your-facial-expressions-to-judge-creditworthiness-b0e9a9ac4174

Global Market Insights (2021). Facial Recognition Market

Size 2020–2026. Global Market Insights. www.gminsights. com/request-sample/detail/2593

Goldstein, A. J., Harmon, L. and Lesk, A. (1971). Identification of human faces. *Proceedings of the IEEE* 59(5): 748–60.

Grafsgaard, J., Wiggins, J., Boyer, K., Wiebe, E. and Lester, J. (2013). Embodied Affect in Tutorial Dialogue: Student Gesture and Posture. *Proceedings of the 16th International Conference on Artificial Intelligence in Education*, 1–10.

Gray, M. (2003). Urban Surveillance and Panopticism. *Surveillance & Society* 1(3): 314–30.

Green, B. (2018). *Data Science as Political Action.* https:// arxiv.org/pdf/1811.03435

Greenfield, A. (2018). *Radical Technologies.* London: Verso.

Guardian (2019). The Guardian View on Facial Recognition. 9 June. *Guardian,* www.theguardian.com/ commentisfree/2019/jun/09/the-guardian-view-on-facial-recognition-a-danger-to-democracy

Guo, E. and Noor, H. (2021). This is the Real Story of the Afghan Biometric Databases Abandoned to the Taliban. *MIT Technology Review*, 30 August. www. technologyreview.com/2021/08/30/1033941/afghanistan-biometric-databases-us-military-40-data-points/

Gurley, L. (2021). Amazon Delivery Drivers Forced to Sign 'Biometric Consent' Form or Lose Job. *Vice*, 21 March. https://www.vice.com/en/article/dy8n3j/amazon-delivery-drivers-forced-to-sign-biometric-consent-form-or-lose-job

Gurovich, Y. et al. (2019). Identifying Facial Phenotypes of Genetic Disorders Using Deep Learning. *Nature Medicine* 25: 60–4.

Haggerty, K. and Ericson, R. (2000). The Surveillant Assemblage. *British Journal of Sociology* 51(4): 605–22.

Hall, R. (2007). Of Ziploc Bags and Black Holes: The Aesthetics of Transparency in the War on Terror. *The Communication Review* 10(4): 319–46.

Hamid, S (2020). Community Defence. *Logic* 11. https:// logicmag.io/care/community-defense-sarah-t-hamid-on-abolishing-carceral-technologies/

Hao, K, (2021). Big Tech's Guide to Talking about AI Ethics. *MIT Technology Review*, 13 April. www.technologyreview. com/2021/04/13/1022568/big-tech-ai-ethics-guide/

Harding, J. (2019). *Are Enemies One Heartbeat Away from Being Found Out?* 1 July. https://toinformistoinfluence. wordpress.com/2019/07/01/are-enemies-one-heartbeat-away-from-being-found-out/

Hartzog, W. and Selinger, E. (2015). Surveillance as Loss of Obscurity. *Washington and Lee Law Review* 72(3): 1343–87.

Harwell, D. (2018). Unproven Facial-Recognition Companies Target Schools. *Washington Post*, 7 June.

Hatch, P. (2019). Underage Gambling? *Sydney Morning Herald*, 26 December. https://www.smh.com.au/business/companies/underage-gambling-tab-s-new-eye-in-the-sky-artificial-intelligence-can-stop-that-20191223-p53mdk. html

Hill, K. (2020). The Secretive Company that Might End Privacy as We Know It. *New York Times*, 18 January. www.nytimes.com/2020/01/18/technology/clearview-privacy-facial-recognition.html

Hill, K. and Mac, R. (2021). Facebook, Citing Societal Concerns, Plans to Shut Down Facial Recognition System. *New York Times*, 2 November. https://www.nytimes.com/2021/11/02/technology/facebook-facial-recognition.html

Hutchins, B. and Andrejevic, M. (2021). Olympian Surveillance. *International Journal of Communication* 15: 363–82.

IBM (2020). *IBM Research Releases 'Diversity in Faces' Dataset to Advance Study of Fairness in Facial Recognition Systems*, 29 January. https://www.ibm.com/blogs/research/2019/01/diversity-in-faces/

Indian Express (2020). Pune: App to Help Cops Track Externed Criminals. *Indian Express*, 15 June. https://indianexpress.com/article/cities/pune/pune-app-to-help-cops-track-externed-criminals-6459272/

Introna, L. and Wood, D. (2004). Picturing Algorithmic Surveillance. *Surveillance & Society* 2(2/3): 177–98.

Jacobsen, K. (2019). New Forms of Intervention. *Handbook on Intervention and Statebuilding*. Edward Elgar Publishing.

Jassy, A. (2019). PBS Frontline interview. https://twitter.com/alfredwkng/status/1356717392961937413

Juniper Research (2020). Juniper Research – 1.3 Billion Smartphones Expected to Feature Software-based Facial Recognition by 2024. *Juniper Research*, 7 January. https://www.juniperresearch.com/press/facial-recognition-hardware-to-feature-on-over-800

Kärkkäinen, K. and Joo, J. (2021). FairFace. *Proceedings of the IEEE/CVF Winter Conference on Applications of Computer Vision*, pp. 1548–58.

Kelly, K. (2019). AR will Spark the Next Big Tech Platform. *Wired*, 12 February. https://www.wired.com/story/mirrorworld-ar-next-big-tech-platform/

Keyes, O., Hitzig, Z. and Blell, M. (2021). Truth from the Machine. *Interdisciplinary Science Reviews* 46(1–2): 158–75.

Khan, N. (2019). Seeing, Naming, Knowing. *The Brooklyn Rail*. March. https://brooklynrail.org/2019/03/art/Seeing-Naming-Knowing

Khoo, L. and Mahmood, M. (2020). Application of Facial Recognition Technology on Identification of the Dead During Large-Scale Disasters. *Forensic Science International: Synergy* 2(3): 238–9.

Knutson, A. (2021). Saving Face: The Unconstitutional Use of Facial Recognition on Undocumented Immigrants and Solutions in IP. *IP Theory* 10(1), Art. 2.

Kohler, M. (2018). Face Recognition, Machine Learning. 17 January. https://maxkoehler.com/posts/2018-01-17-feret-database/

Kopstein, J. (2017). DHS Face Recognition Tech Could See Through Car Windows. *Vocativ*, 7 June. www.vocativ.com/news/436639/dhs-face-recognition-automobile-windows/index.html

Kosinski, M. and Wang, Y. (2017). Deep Neural Networks are More Accurate than Humans at Detecting Sexual

Orientation from Facial Images. *Journal of Personality and Social Psychology* 114(2): 246–57.

Lee-Morrison, L. (2019). *Portraits of Automated Facial Recognition.* Verlag. https://library.oapen.org/bitstream/handle/20.500.12657/23435/9783839448465.pdf?sequence=1

Leslie, S. (1993). *The Cold War and American Science.* Columbia University Press.

Liaw, H., Chiu, M. and Chou, C. (2014). Using Facial Recognition Technology in the Exploration of Student Responses to Conceptual Conflict Phenomenon. *Chemistry Education Research and Practice* 15(4): 824–34.

Lyon, D. (2002). Surveillance Studies. *Surveillance & Society* 1(1): 1–7.

Lyon, D. (2015). *Surveillance after Snowden.* Polity Press.

Madianou, M. (2019). Technocolonialism. *Social Media+ Society* 5(3): 1–13.

Magnet, S. (2011). *When Biometrics Fail: Gender, Race, and Technology of Identity.* Duke University Press.

Mateescu, A. and Elish, M. (2019). AI in Context. *Data & Society.* https://datasociety.net/library/ai-in-context/

Mayer, J. (2013). What's the Matter with Metadata? *New Yorker*, 6 June. www.newyorker.com/news/news-desk/whats-the-matter-with-metadata

Menegus, B. (2019). Defence of Amazon's Face Recognition Tool Undermined by its Only Known Police Client. *Gizmodo*, 31 January.

Metz, R. (2021). Anyone Can Use This Powerful Facial-Recognition Tool – and That's a Problem. 4 May, *CNN Business*.

Montgomery, J. and Marais, A. (2014). Educational Content Access Control System. *US Patent Application* 14/212,069, filed 18 September.

Mozur, P. (2019a). One Month, 500,000 Face Scans. *New York Times*, 15 April. https://www.nytimes.com/2019/04/14/technology/china-surveillance-artificial-intelligence-racial-profiling.html

Mozur, P. (2019b). In Hong Kong Protests, Faces Become Weapons. *New York Times*, 26 July. https://www.nytimes.com/2019/07/26/technology/hong-kong-protests-facial-recognition-surveillance.html

National Review (2019). Facial-Recognition Technology. *National Review*, 25 November. www.nationalreview.com/2019/11/facial-recognition-technology-closer-to-utopia-than-dystopia/

Nature (2020). Facial-Recognition Research Needs an Ethical Reckoning. *Nature*, 18 November. www.nature.com/articles/d41586-020-03256-7

New York Times (2001). Giving Web a Memory Cost Its Users Privacy, 4 September. www.nytimes.com/2001/09/04/business/giving-web-a-memory-cost-its-users-privacy.html

New York Times (2008). Recognizing Stripes, Not Faces, Software Tracks Whale Sharks, 1 January. https://www.nytimes.com/2008/01/01/science/01obshar.html

New York Times (2020a). A Case for Banning Facial Recognition, 15 June. https://www.nytimes.com/2020/11/11/technology/facial-recognition-software-police.html

New York Times (2020b). I Could Solve Most of Your Problems, 2 May. www.nytimes.com/2020/05/02/technology/eric-schmidt-pentagon-google.html

Ng, A. (2021). This Manual for a Popular Facial Recognition Tool Shows Just How Much the Software Tracks People. *The MarkUp*, July 6. https://themarkup.org/privacy/2021/07/06/this-manual-for-a-popular-facial-recognition-tool-shows-just-how-much-the-software-tracks-people

Noll, R. (2003). Federal R&D in the Antiterrorist Era. *Innovation Policy and the Economy* 3: 61–89.

Nordmann, A. (2007). If and Then. *Nanoethics* 1(1): 31–46.

Norris, S. (2019). And the Eye in the Sky is Watching Us All. *UNLV Gaming Law Journal* 9: 269–91.

Offert, F. and Bell, P. (2020). Perceptual Bias and Technical Metapictures: Critical Machine Vision as a Humanities

Challenge. *AI & Society* 36: 1133–44. https://doi.
org/10.1007/s00146-020-01058-z

Office of the Privacy Commissioner of Canada (2021).
Clearview AI's Unlawful Practices Represented Mass
Surveillance of Canadians, Commissioners Say. Press
release, 3 February. https://www.priv.gc.ca/en/opc-news/
news-and-announcements/2021/nr-c_210203/

O'Neill, J. (2019). How Facial Recognition Makes You
Safer. *New York Times*, 9 June. https://www.nytimes.
com/2019/06/09/opinion/facial-recognition-police-new-
york-city.html

Pasquale, F. (2020) *New Laws of Robotics: Defending Human
Expertise in the Age of AI*. Harvard University Press.

Petkoff, P. (2012). Forum Internum and Forum Externum
in Canon Law and Public International Law. *Religion &
Human Rights* 7(3): 183–214.

Phillips, P., Rauss, P. and Der, S. (1996). *FERET (Face
Recognition Technology) Recognition Algorithm
Development and Test Results*. https://www.nist.gov/
system/files/documents/2021/04/27/feret3.pdf

PimEyes (2022). How It Works: Protect Your Privacy. https://
pimeyes.com/en

Pivcevic, K. (2021). Biometrics Planned for AnyVision
JV's First Drones for Military Use. *Biometric Update*, 4
January. www.biometricupdate.com/202101/biometrics-
planned-for-anyvision-jvs-first-drones-for-military-use

Raji, D. (2021). Tweet, 24 April. https://twitter.com/rajiinio/
status/1385935151981420557

Raviv, S. (2020). The Secret History of Facial Recognition.
Wired, 21 January.

Rogoway, M. (2020). Intel Starts Using Facial Recognition
Technology to ID Workers, Visitors. *The Oregonian*, 11
March.

Rosen, J. (2011). *The Unwanted Gaze*. Vintage.

Rouvroy, A. and Berns, T. (2013). Gouvernementalité
algorithmique et perspectives d'émancipation. *Réseaux* 1:
163–96.

SAFR (2020). *Casinos, Face Recognition, and COVID-19: Six Questions with Sam Kljajic.* 15 April. https://safr.com/general/ask-the-expert-casinos-face-recognition-and-covid-19/

Schneier, B. (2003). *Beyond Fear.* Copernicus Books.

Sekula, A. (1986). The Body and the Archive. *October* 39: 3–64.

Senftt, T. (2019). Tweet. https://twitter.com/terrisenft/status/1204561759605940224

Shwayder, M. (2020). Clearview AI's Facial-Recognition App is a Nightmare for Stalking Victims. *Digital Trends*, 22 January. www.digitaltrends.com/news/clearview-ai-facial-recognition-domestic-violence-stalking/

SIA (2020). US Public Opinion Research on the Support of Facial Recognition, 18 September. www.securityindustry.org/report/u-s-public-opinion-research-on-the-support-of-facial-recognition/

SIA (2021). Facial Recognition. www.securityindustry.org/advocacy/policy-priorities/facial-recognition/

Simon, M. (2009). HP Looking into Claim Webcams Can't See Black People. *CNN,* 24 December. https://edition.cnn.com/2009/TECH/12/22/hp.webcams/index.html

Singh, R. (2019). Give Me a Database and I Will Raise the Nation-State. *South Asia: Journal of South Asian Studies* 42(3): 501–18.

Sirovich, L. and Kirby, M. (1987). Low-Dimensional Procedure for the Characterization of Human Faces. *Journal for the Optical Society of America A* 4(3): 519–24.

Smyth, J. (2021). States Push Back Against Use of Facial Recognition by Police. *ABC News*, 6 May. https://abcnews.go.com/Politics/wireStory/states-push-back-facial-recognition-police-77510175

Solon, O. (2019). Facial Recognition's 'Dirty Little Secret'. *NBC News*, 12 March. www.nbcnews.com/tech/internet/facial-recognition-s-dirty-little-secret-millions-online-photos-scraped-n981921

Stark, L. (2019). Facial Recognition is the Plutonium of AI. *XRDS – Crosswords* (ACM), April.

Steinberger, M. (2020). Does Palantir See Too Much? *New York Times*, 21 October. https://cacm.acm.org/news/248353-does-palantir-see-too-much/fulltext

Stevens, N. and Keyes, O. (2021). Seeing Infrastructure. *Cultural Studies* 35(4–5): 833–53.

Stirrat, M., Stulp, G. and Pollet, T. (2012). Male Facial Width is Associated with Death by Contact Violence. *Evolution and Human Behavior* 33: 551–6.

Swanlund, D. and Schuurman, N. (2018). Second Generation Biometrics and the Future of Geosurveillance. *ACME: An International Journal for Critical Geographies* 17(4): 920–38.

Taylor, A. (2018). The Automation Charade. *Logic*, 1 August. https://logicmag.io/failure/the-automation-charade/

Taylor, J. (2021). 7-Eleven Took Photos of Some Australian Customers' Faces without Consent, Privacy Commissioner Rules. *Guardian*, 14 October. www.theguardian.com/australia-news/2021/oct/14/7-eleven-took-photos-of-some-australian-customers-faces-without-consent-privacy-commissioner-rules

Timms, M. (2016). Letting Artificial Intelligence in Education Out of the Box. *International Journal of Artificial Intelligence in Education* 26(2): 701–12.

Tucker, P. (2019). Here Come AI-Enabled Cameras Meant to Sense Crime Before It Occurs. *Defence One*, 24 April. www.defenseone.com/technology/2019/04/ai-enabled-cameras-detect-crime-it-occurs-will-soon-invade-physical-world/156502/

Turk, M. and Pentland, A. (1991). Eigenfaces for Recognition. *Journal of Cognitive Neuroscience* 3(1): 71–86.

UNICEF (2019) *Faces, Fingerprints and Feet*. UNICEF.

US Chamber of Commerce (2019). Coalition Letter on Facial Recognition Technology, 16 October. https://www.uschamber.com/letters-congress/coalition-letter-facial-recognition-technology

Valentino-DeVries, J. (2020). How the Police Use Facial Recognition, and Where it Falls Short. *New York Times*, 12 January. https://www.nytimes.com/2020/01/12/technology/facial-recognition-police.html

Valera, J., Valera, J. and Gelogo, Y. (2015). A Review on Facial Recognition for Online Learning Authentication. *Eighth International Conference on Bio-Science and Bio-Technology (BSBT)*. IEEE, pp. 16–19.

Vincent, J. (2021). The EU is Considering a Ban on AI for Mass Surveillance and Social Credit Scores. *The Verge*, 14 April. www.theverge.com/2021/4/14/22383301/eu-ai-regulation-draft-leak-surveillance-social-credit

Viola, P. and Jones, M. (2001). Robust Real-Time Object Detection. *International Journal of Computer Vision* 57(2): 137–54.

Virilio, P. (2007 [1998]). Surfing the Accident: interview for '*The Art of the Accident*'. https://v2.nl/archive/articles/surfing-the-accident

Wagh, P., Thakare, R., Chaudhari, J. and Patil, S. (2015). Attendance System Based on Face Recognition Using Eigen Face and PCA Algorithms. *2015 International Conference on Green Computing and Internet of Things (ICGCIoT)*. IEEE, pp. 303–8.

Wajcman, J. (2019). The Digital Architecture of Time Management. *Science, Technology and Human Values* 44(2): 315–37.

Wang, C., Zhang, Q., Liu, W., Liu, Y. and Miao, L. (2018). Facial Feature Discovery for Ethnicity Recognition. *Wiley Interdisciplinary Reviews: Data Mining and Knowledge Discovery* 9(1): e1278.

Watts, R. (2019). Facial Recognition as a Force for Good. *Biometric Technology Today 2019*(3): 5–8.

Webber, A. (2020). PwC Facial Recognition Tool Criticised for Home Working Privacy Invasion. *Personnel Today*, 16 June.

Weinberger, S. (2010). Airport Security: Intent to Deceive? *Nature*, 26 May. www.nature.com/news/2010/100526/full/465412a.html

Weizman, E. (2012). *Hollow Land*. Verso.

Wen, Y., Raj, B. and Singh, R. (2019). Face Reconstruction from Voice Using Generative Adversarial Networks. *Advances in Neural Information Processing Systems* 32.

Wiewiórowski, W. (2019). *Facial Recognition: A Solution in Search of a Problem?* 28 October. https://edps.europa.eu/press-publications/press-news/blog/facial-recognition-solution-search-problem_en

Winner, L. (1986). *The Whale and the Reactor*. University of Chicago Press.

World Bank (2017). 1.1 Billion 'Invisible' People Without ID Are Priority for New High Level Advisory Council on Identification for Development. Press release, 12 October. www.worldbank.org/en/news/press-release/2017/10/12/11-billion-invisible-people-without-id-are-priority-for-new-high-level-advisory-council-on-identification-for-development

Wu, X. and Zhang, X. (2016). Machine Learning of Criminality Perceptions. https://arxiv.org/abs/1611.04135

Zharovskikh, A. (2020). Facial Recognition for Healthcare Disruption. *InData Labs*, 20 July. https://indatalabs.com/blog/ai-face-recognition-in-healthcare

Žižek, S. (2020). *The Parallax View*. MIT Press.

Zuboff, S. (2019). *The Age of Surveillance Capitalism*. Profile Books.

Index